BRITISH SHORTHAIR CAT

Esther Verhoef

BRITISH SHORTHAIR CAT

REBO
PUBLISHERS

© 2001 Zuid Boekprodukties
© 2006 Rebo Publishers

Text and photographs: Esther Verhoef
Illustrations: Rod Ferring
Reproduction: Minkowsky Graphics, Enkhuizen, The Netherlands
Typesetting and pre-press services: AdAm Studio, Prague, The Czech Republic
Translation: Anthea Bell for First Edition Translations Ltd, Cambridge, UK
Editing: First Edition Translations Ltd, Cambridge, UK
Proofreading: Sarah Dunham

ISBN 13: 978-90-366-1097-1
ISBN 10: 90-366-1097-4

CONTENTS

P. 7: Well-to-do English enthusiasts began taking their cats to shows at the end of the nineteenth century

1 THE HISTORY OF THE BRITISH SHORTHAIR CAT

The earliest pedigree cats

Members of the more prosperous social classes in Britain began showing and breeding cats at the end of the nineteenth century. These animals were mainly cats which they had brought back from their travels, for instance long-haired cats from the Middle and Far East (the ancestors of today's Persian or longhair cats) and exotic shorthairs such as the Siamese, Abyssinian, and Russian Blue. Native cats – the shorthaired British domestic cat and the tailless Manx from the neighbouring Isle of Man – were also shown, but Persians were in the greatest demand. Around the turn of the century the Persian was so popular that scarcely any shorthaired breeds appeared at cat shows, and even if they were entered they hardly ever won awards. Any honors which went to shorthairs tended to be reserved for the exotic-looking Siamese.

The first pedigree cat club

Leading figures in the cat world of the time deplored this state

Black silver tabby British Shorthair of around the turn of the twentieth century

Persians, 1900

of affairs, for ownership of expensive pedigree animals was the perquisite of the better-off. Ordinary folk had to make do with British shorthaired cats, and since the earnings of the working classes were usually low there was not much enthusiasm among them for breeding and showing these animals. The elite of the cat fancy, however, were anxious to involve the less privileged in their hobby, since if they too could win prizes with their domestic cats their interest was sure to be good for the welfare of cats in general. In addition, the people of the United Kingdom of that time were not devoid of chauvinism, and were naturally

Maria, a British Shorthair female of around the turn of the twentieth century

keen to see their native cats bred to standards of beauty which would enable them to compete with foreign cats. It was time to lend the British shorthaired domestic cat more status. The result was the founding of the first pedigree club for native shorthaired cats, which is still in existence today; the Short Haired Cat Society and Manx Club came into existence in 1901. The club was represented at a number of cat shows. It gave awards for the best native shorthaired cats, and in this way more interest began to be aroused in the English shorthaired domestic cat.

From domestic cat to pedigree cat
The British domestic cat, usually known at the time as the Shorthair or the English (or British) cat, had many different forms and colors, because it had never been methodically bred. It was difficult to assess and compare the cats for their beauty because there were no standards. A pedigree standard was therefore drawn up, describing the ideal outward appearance of the new British Shorthair breed. Among other points, it specified that the cats should have the physical build of the sturdily built Persian, but with a shorthaired coat. Breeders

Champion Xenophon, a black blotched or classic tabby British Shorthair who lived at the end of the nineteenth century

began selecting cats for a compact, substantial build with a dense, shorthaired, plushy coat, sometimes crossing their shorthairs with Persians to accelerate this development.
Equally important were the coat colors that the cats were required to have for admittance to cat shows. The only permissible colors were self blue, black, and white; black, red, and silver tabby; tortoiseshell, tortie and white, and tabby and white. The correct tabby patterns and eye colors, the depth and precise hue of the coat colors, and the arrangement of any markings were clearly set out in an appendix to the breed standard which described colors. In this way a stage was ultimately reached where a properly bred shorthair could be distinguished from a domestic cat born from a random mating, and evidence of the success of

that development exists in the many award-winning cats of the past and present.

Europe

Nor was it the English alone who put their minds to breeding and showing cats, although their influence was certainly of great importance. An interest in pedigree cats began to arise in mainland Europe, where breeders also wanted to breed luxury pedigree animals from the existing farm cats of their own countries. These cats, known at first as European Shorthairs, were of very much the same type as those being bred in the United Kingdom under the name of British Shorthairs. European cat associations adopted the breed standard of the British cats for their own Continental variants, and animals were also regularly imported from the United Kingdom to introduce new bloodlines. The result, in the long term, was a breeding stock of shorthaired pedigree cats identical in both outward appearance and ancestry on both sides of the English Channel.

British Shorthair versus European Shorthair

In northern Europe, however, the situation was different. Breeders in Scandinavia were also concentrating on the selective breeding of sturdy domestic cats, and these cats too were shown under the breed name of European Shorthairs. But the Scandinavian cats were of a rather different type from the European Shorthairs because Scandinavian

Blue British Shorthair

Until 1973 it was possible to register any domestic cat as a British Shorthair so long as it conformed to the breed type.

Around 1900 this spotted pattern was regarded as ideal

breeders imported far fewer British animals, and their stock was based to a greater extent on sturdy local domestic cats. In addition, they did not practise any outcrossing with Persians, and as a result problems arose when cat fancy became more international. It was a question of the existence of two breeds of different appearance for which, however, there was only one standard and one breed name. In the 1980s, therefore, a distinction was drawn at the request of breeders in Scandinavia. Cobbily built animals with Persian in their ancestry were to be known as British Shorthairs, while the breed name European Shorthair was reserved for the rather less cobby animals of more or less pure descent from European domestic cats. In addition, the French Chartreux, a blue self cat which had hitherto been placed in the same category, also acquired separate breed status. The Chartreux is not very widely bred at present, and neither is the European Shorthair, but today the British Shorthair has become one of the most popular of all cat breeds.

P. 13:
A black
silver tabby male
with an imposing
head

2 PHYSICAL CHARACTER-ISTICS

The breed standard

The breed standard of the British Shorthair is one of the few pedigree standards to have remained practically identical all over the world in every national cat association. The original standard, from which all others derive, is that of the British organization, the Governing Council of the Cat Fancy (GCCF). The GCCF standard of points is given below.

Type

The British Cat is compact, well-balanced and powerful, showing good depth of body, a full broad chest, short legs, rounded paws, tail thick at base with rounded tip. The head is round with good width between small ears, round cheeks, firm chin, large round and well-opened eyes and a short broad nose. The coat is short and dense.

Head

A round face with full cheeks and good breadth of skull with a round underlying bone structure. The head should be set on a short thick neck. Nose: the nose itself should be short, broad and straight. In profile, a rounded forehead should lead to

*Young lilac male
with a handsome,
compact body build*

Above left:
Lilac tortie queen
(female); queens
are smaller than
males and do not
have such massive
heads

Above right:
Black tortie and
white female with
the correct sturdy
build

a short straight nose with a nose break which is neither too pronounced nor too shallow. Chin: a strong, firm, and deep chin is essential. Any deviation from this is to be considered a fault. The bite must be level, the tip of the chin to line up with the tip of the nose in the same vertical plane. Ears: small, rounded at the tips. Set far apart, fitting into (without distorting) the rounded contour of the head. External ear to be well-covered with fur, internal furnishings not to be excessive. Eyes: large, round, and well-opened. Set wide apart with no tendency to Oriental shape. No squint.

Body

Cobby type with short level back. Low on legs with deep chest. Equally massive across the shoulders and the rump. Medium to large, but not rangy. Legs and paws: short, strong legs. Paws round and firm. Tail: should be thick and of medium length, thicker at the base with rounded tip.

Coat

Must be short, dense and crisp. A soft and/or overlong and fluffy coat is incorrect.

Condition

Perfect physical condition and an alert, vital appearance.

Faults

Malformations of the jaw or mouth, malformations of the tail and any other anatomical deviation; overlong or soft, fluffy coat; fluffy tail; pronounced nose stop; weak chin; pronounced whisker pads. Withholding faults (i.e. a first place or challenge certificate cannot be awarded): uneven bite; deviation of bone structure of the tail or other physical malformation; overlong or fluffy coat (in adults); pronounced nose stop, flat face or snub nose.

Colors and the standard

The breed standard for type and build is practically identical for all British Shorthairs worldwide, but the same is not true of the various combinations of colors and markings, which can differ from one country or organization to another. These recognized combinations, however, are not rigidly established, since breeders are always working on new ways of improving and refining the breed. Such developments do not proceed at the same pace all over the world, and consequently the recognition of (new) color groups can vary between countries and organizations.

Later chapters describe the British Shorthair color groups, but because of the many variations in their recognition from country to country this book may not necessarily be absolutely up to date in stating whether a certain color is or is not recognized – and by which organization. The aim has been to give an account of the best-known colors and color groups. A list of all the colors at present being bred and shown will be found in Chapter 16.

A fine blue male

P. 17:
British Shorthair
kitten, black silver
shell

3 FIRST CONSIDERA-TIONS

The pros and cons

You will already have thought about the pleasures of keeping a British Shorthair as a domestic pet. But acquiring a living creature means that you have responsibilities to it as well. A healthy, carefully bred British Shorthair can easily live to the age of fifteen years, and every day of its life the cat will be entirely dependent on you for food, care and attention. You will not only have to clean out the litter tray every day, you must provide the cat with a well-balanced diet, which unfortunately does not come cheap. "Regular maintenance" such as worming, flea control, and annual booster inoculations against panleucopaenia (infectious enteritis) and feline upper respiratory tract disease (cat flu) are all part of the routine care of a cat. Adult British Shorthairs are generally quite placid, but young animals in particular may easily knock over a pretty plant container or dig their claws into the three-piece suit. In addition, a cat – old or young, male or female – may sometimes urinate in the wrong place or bring up a hairball on the carpet. Like all cats, a British Shorthair will moult. Of course it should be brushed or combed daily in the moulting season, but you will still keep

British Shorthair
kittens can be
mischievous

finding its hairs on your furniture and clothes. And when you go on holiday you will either have to find someone to look after your cat while you are away or look for a good cattery.

It is to be hoped that your cat will not fall sick or have an accident, but these things happen, and once again the cat is entirely dependent on your care. Consulting a veterinarian can be quite expensive, and you may have to take a day or two off work to look after your sick pet. Cats, like ourselves, suffer the infirmities of old age, and your British Shorthair will probably need extra care in the later years of its life.

All this is part of keeping a cat as a pet, so it is important for you to be well aware of all the "cons" as well as the "pros" before you take a kitten or an adult cat into your household.

Kittens with character

The great majority of people choose a kitten rather than a fully grown cat. This is very understandable: kittens are irresistible, and British Shorthair kittens, with their rounded, cuddly appearance, are the most appealing of all. But you might still prefer to choose a rather older cat. The bond you create between yourself and an adult cat is just as strong as the bond you form with a kitten. An older cat may take longer than a kitten to get used to its new home, but in the end it will frequently settle down just as well. Some people get a kitten because they think they can then form its character to suit themselves. However, the character of a cat depends partly on its heredity, partly on the environment in which it grew up as a kitten, and the breeder's attitude to his or her cats. All you can do yourself is to add the finishing touches and teach the kitten the rules of your own home.

Kittens of all breeds are appealing, but British Shorthair kittens are irresistible

Getting an adult cat

For some people a rather older cat which has already had a good home somewhere else can be a better choice – for instance if you work outside your home, and cannot keep a kitten company and bring it up satisfactorily in the first months of its life with you. Many pedigree cat clubs have someone who deals with the re-homing of adult cats of the breed. You should listen to such people's advice and be straightforward with them: they will love the breed concerned, and do not deserve a disappointment after trying to find a cat a good home.

An older cat sometimes takes longer to settle in

By no means all adult cats in need of new homes are "problem cases." There can be all kinds of reasons why people have to give up their pets: divorce or illness, for instance, or the owner's death. The fact that it has to be re-homed tells you nothing about the cat itself. It is different when a cat has to be re-homed because he or she is aggressive, excessively timid, chronically dirty in its habits, or either cannot or will not get along with other pets. Although such cats quite often stop showing these negative characteristics in a new home, you have to be careful with them. Suitable arrangements have to be made in case the older cat has problems settling down in your home. If you do not know a great deal about cats yourself, it is a good idea to find someone who does have a good knowledge of the subject and ask about the breeder.

Male or female?

The most striking difference between male and female British Shorthairs is their appearance. The males of the breed are more imposing in every respect than their female counterparts. However, their characters are very similar: some males are friendly and some less friendly, and the same is true of females.

If you are not planning to breed, then the choice between a male and a female is a matter of personal preference. However, if you want to raise a litter of kittens then of course you will want a breeding queen.

It is almost impossible to keep male cats indoors for long periods because they spray. However, if you do not want to breed but would like to show your cat, you may be interested to know that male and female neuters can be shown as well as entire cats. They are entered and judged in separate classes of their own.

If you have a cat already

If you already have one or more cats, then perhaps you should ask yourself if your other cats will accept the newcomer easily. That will depend on yourself – can you keep calm and be patient? – the character of your existing cat or cats, and the character of the new pet. Even-tempered, easy-going cats who have had plenty of interaction with other cats in their youth, and perhaps later, seldom cause any problems when a new companion is introduced into the home. In such cases the newcomer is often fully accepted within one or two weeks. However, some cats are not happy to share their homes, and may make this clear by developing dirty habits or becoming nervous, withdrawing to a quiet place in the house and refus-

A kitten is often quickly accepted without any problems

ing food, or simply by showing constant hostility to the new-comer. Sometimes the dark clouds may disperse, given time, but in some cases if the situation does not improve it may be better to re-home one of the cats.

A kitten is usually much more readily accepted by an existing group of cats, but one cannot take that for granted. Just like human beings, cats can take a liking or dislike to each other, and it is not always easy to tell in advance on which side the balance will come down. An adult British Shorthair which got on well with other cats when living with its previous owner will not usually cause problems in your own household. When you first bring the new cat home it is a good idea to let it explore your house for a few hours before introducing it to the other cats.

Living with dogs

Cats, either young or old, who have had a good start in life with their breeders or owners generally settle down easily in a household with other pets. If you have a dog who is used to cats and treats them with respect, it will normally accept the newcomer too. But even if your dog does chase cats outside the home, that does not necessarily mean it will treat your new pet in the same way. A great many dogs chase strange cats, but will not touch the familiar cat they know at home.

Nonetheless, a certain amount of caution is advisable, particularly if you have a rather aggressive dog. You have to know your dog well to predict how he or she will react to a cat. It goes without saying that you will not leave the cat and dog alone together in the early stages, and that the cat must have satisfactory boltholes – places where the dog cannot follow it. You

A well-socialized British Shorthair can get on very well with dogs

can also help the animals to get on with each other by giving your dog a piece of cheese or meat whenever the cat is around; in that way it will associate the presence of the new cat with a treat.

Sometimes it is easier to take an older cat who is already used to dogs into your home. Mewing, playful kittens running about can occasionally bring out the hunting instinct in certain dogs.

Cats and children

Many families acquire a pet because the children are so keen to have one. It is very good for children's social development to grow up with animals, learning to take the responsibility for a living creature at times. However, young children should not be expected to shoulder the whole burden of caring for the cat.

A cat flap is very useful if your cat is to go in and out as it likes

Children have not yet developed a full sense of responsibility, and with a few exceptions the novelty of the new pet soon wears off, so care of the cat will ultimately be up to you. Assuming that your British Shorthair may live for fifteen years, it is not out of the question that the children will have left home when the cat is still in the prime of life. So do not get a cat solely for the children; you yourself must welcome the idea of a cat in the home. Of course you will teach your children that the cat is a living creature which deserves respect, and that neither kittens nor adult cats ever like to have their sleep disturbed. It goes without saying that you must never allow the children to be too rough with their pet, or chase it all over the house with loud shouts. This kind of thing can upset cats so much that, depending on their character, they become either timid or aggressive out of fear.

An only cat

Contrary to popular opinion, cats are not solitary animals: that is true only of cats who grow up in the wild. Their mother teaches them to stand on their own feet at a definite time: she stops feeding her kittens and caring for the litter when they are about eleven weeks old, making them independent of her within a relatively short period, and they grow up as fairly solitary animals. However, a kitten born among human beings as a domesticated cat never suffers repudiation. We go on grooming the cat's coat by stroking and brushing it, we provide it with food, and by doing so we are imitating the care a mother cat gives her kittens. Through our good offices, the mentality of the domestic cat remains to a great extent stuck at the "kitten stage," and at that stage it feels a great need for company, including the company of its own kind. If you get a British Shorthair kitten and then leave it to its own devices for most of the day, it will grow up socially deprived, so if you cannot offer your new pet enough attention and social interaction yourself, you should get two cats. Then they will have someone to "talk to" while you are out.

If you do not have another cat already and you are out at work all day, it is better to get two cats to keep each other company

Freedom beckons, but it is full of dangers

Indoor cat or outdoor cat?

British Shorthairs are mainly placid by nature, and some own-ers prefer to keep them as indoor cats. They do not need to go out of doors to be happy, but of course they must be provided with means of scratching, climbing, and playing, and they need to get enough exercise.

Allowing cat free access to the outside world entails certain risks. Not only can it be infected with serious feline diseases, but – depending on where you live – it also runs the risk of a road accident, a confrontation with a ferocious dog, or poisoning. There is also the strong likelihood that a cat allowed to go where it likes will relieve itself in your neighbors' garden and cause bad feeling. And finally, since British Shorthairs are attractive,

A friendly meeting between two cats of the same breed

friendly animals, there is always a risk that your pet will be picked up and taken home by someone else. Nevertheless, many owners feel that it is a cat's right to roam freely and hunt for prey.

Runs and screens

If you decide to keep your cat permanently indoors, fix stout screens over the window frames. Then you can let air into the house, but the cat cannot run away. Keep it in from kitten age onwards so that it does not get used to outdoors. Neutered British Shorthairs who have never been used to going out from their early weeks of life will not feel the urge to do so during their adult lives, a very convenient arrangement.

If you have a garden you can make a cat run with your back door or a window leading into it. Another possibility is a stout fence round the garden, with a wire charged with a weak electric current above it, or a high trellis bent over at the top. This will effectively discourage most British Shorthairs. A balcony can be fenced in with stout wire netting so that the cat can go out on it safely, and a cat flap in the door will allow it to come in and go out as it pleases.

Will a British Shorthair be right for me?

A British Shorthair usually has an equable temper and a placid, amiable character. A well- socialized cat with the nature typical of the breed will generally get on well with other cats, with dogs, and with children.

British Shorthairs like to interact a great deal with "their" humans. They enjoy being stroked and cuddled, but seldom force their attentions on people, although there are exceptions. In their youth they are often very playful, but they become less active when they are around two years old. The cats can keep themselves occupied relatively well, but they are sociable ani-

Above left:
An outside run
need not cost
a great deal, and
it will give your
British Shorthair
the chance to get
fresh air safely.

Above right:
A safely enclosed
garden will
ensure that your
British Shorthair
stays on its own
territory.

Like most British Shorthairs, this lilac male is a real sybarite.

mals and like company – a British Shorthair is not a cat that can happily spend the day alone. It will probably not protest by vandalizing the furniture, but it will have less *joie de vivre*, and will show it in subtler ways.

These qualities, and the fact that British Shorthairs are not as "talkative" as, for instance, many breeds of Oriental origin, make them good cats for quiet people and busy families alike. However, some British Shorthairs do have more complex characters, so in order to avoid disappointment it is important that you do not simply buy the first kitten you see.

Bi-color black and white male

Above:
Lilac colorpointed
female

Left:
Black silver shad-
ed kitten

P. 29:
*No breeder can
ever guarantee that
your kitten will
grow up to be
a champion.*

4 BUYING A KITTEN

Cats sold without pedigree certificates

The British Shorthair is a popular breed. Blue was the color most sought after for years, but recently the silver tabby has been in great demand because of its frequent appearance in advertising campaigns. It is precisely because of its popularity that you must be particularly alert when you are looking for a British Shorthair kitten. Kittens (including silver tabbies) may sometimes be offered for sale without pedigree papers. These animals are almost never pure-bred; they are usually domestic cats which resemble silver tabbies, or are the result of a cross between a Persian and a domestic cat.

Even if a litter does in fact seem to be genuinely pure-bred, a pedigree cat without its papers is always suspect. The cost of registering a pedigree cat does not on average amount to as much as four percent of the usual sale price of a kitten, and if the breeder knows his or her business, there is no reason at all why a cat association should decline to issue pedigree registration forms. A few associations do so, but only when the parents of a litter have not been tested (or have tested positive) for infections and diseases which may prove fatal in the future, such as feline AIDS and feline leukaemia. Another instance in which an association may decide not to register pedigree kittens is when the breeder is letting a queen have more litters than is good for her – three litters in two years is normally the maximum. You will see by now that you would do better not to follow up offers of kittens from litters without pedigree certificates – there is usually something wrong with them.

A show cat

If you want to show and/or breed from your new pet, it is sensible not to go out in search of available kittens straight away; you should get to know all you can about the breed first. Not every kitten is suitable for showing and/or breeding, and not every breeder is automatically an expert on all aspects of the breed – in particular the good and less good qualities of the parents and other ancestors, and of the available kittens themselves.

You should buy a kitten for showing or breeding only from an experienced, well-known breeder with a good reputation. Generally you can get in touch with such breeders through the information on kitten availability issued by a cat club, or even better through a specialist breed club. When you are telephoning with your enquiries, you should make it perfectly clear what you are looking for.

Since you may want to breed from your kitten, it is important for

you to find a breeder who has his or her kittens checked for those hereditary faults which can occur in British Shorthairs. Another important point is to ascertain that there are no cats of any other breed among the ancestors of your British Shorthair, perhaps with the exception of a single Persian some way back in the past. Do not feel awkward about visiting a number of different breeders so that you can compare them. Then you will be able to make a judicious decision and go ahead to buy from the breeder whose treatment of his or her cats, knowledge of the breed, and naturally whose cats themselves appeal to you most. None the less, no breeder, however experienced, can guarantee that your kitten will grow up to be a champion. All the breeder can do is help you to find a kitten of excellent ancestry which, even while very young, shows promise because it has the right color, coat texture, markings, and specific physical characteristics typical of the breed. For instance, British Shorthair kittens may look very promising with their chunky, compact build in youth, but it is not always possible to say whether they will still be like that when they grow up.

A British Shorthair as a pet

If you are looking for a British Shorthair as a pet, and are not planning to breed from the cat or show it, small faults may be less important to you. You can afford to be rather less critical about the cat's appearance. Every litter contains one or more kittens which the breeder can see will not come up to the high requirements of the breed standard. Examples are bi-color British Shorthairs with too little white for the standard, or cats

Bi-colors with too little white in their markings are often sold at a lower price, but as domestic pets they are in no way inferior to their show-quality siblings.

which look as if they will not have the desired eye color, or which show insufficient contrast in a tabby pattern. These kittens are usually sold as "pet quality," generally at a lower price than those of show or breeding quality. Sometimes two British Shorthair parents can produce a longhaired kitten. Such kittens have just the same good background as the show quality kittens in their litter, so you can be sure of buying a cat which is perfectly alright otherwise.

Some breeders ask you to sign a form stating that you will have the male or female with "faults" neutered at the right time. This is the breeder's way of ensuring that the faults (or poor colors) will not be passed on to subsequent generations.

The litter must be reared in hygienic surroundings.

What should I look for?

When you go to see a breeder and meet the kittens, there are a number of things to look out for. Most breeders have several cats in the house, and sometimes in a run outside as well, but it is not a good sign if the place is positively swarming with cats. Cats need care and attention, and when there are too many in the house they can never all get enough of that attention. The kittens ought to be reared indoors in the house, not in a shed or outdoor run, where they may have problems in developing social skills. Mentally and physically healthy kittens will see your visit as a welcome diversion in the usual routine of their day, and if they are wide awake they should find it very interesting and not at all alarming. You should also check the hygiene of the household. A cattery may not smell quite as fresh as your own home, especially when there are unneutered or "entire" males in the house or in a nearby stud house. However, there is no excuse for litter trays full of feces and other signs betraying a below-average standard of care.

If all this is in order, then see if the kittens give the impression of good health. Runny nose or eyes, fleas in the coat, dirty ears, or traces of diarrhea are not good signs. Do not buy kittens with

There can be no better way of developing social skills; these kittens are perfectly at ease with the family dog.

these symptoms, which indicate that they may be suffering from some sickness. Other signs of something not quite right are over-round stomachs and bare patches in the kitten's coat, for which there may be various undesirable causes. In such cases, which are fortunately rare, you should never visit another cattery on the same day because of the danger of bringing infection into it.

Your choice

If it is a pet cat you want, choose the kitten which appeals to you most. Cats have their own preferences too, and there is a strong likelihood that one of the kittens will show that it has taken to you. Instinctive likings often turn out well. Whatever you do, it is better not to choose the "misfit" in the litter, even if it seems cheap. There is often a good reason for a kitten's poor condition, and if you buy it you may well have saddled yourself with emotional as well as financial problems. If you want a kitten for

It is difficult for the uninitiated to choose between kittens, but the breeder can tell you which shows promise.

P. 33: Blue color-pointed kitten

showing or breeding, it is a good idea to take the breeder's advice. But whatever the cat's outward appearance, it is going to be part of your household for the next fifteen years, so it is very important for the two of you to like each other. If the prettiest kitten has a temperament which does not appeal to you, you would do better to wait for another litter to be born.

Taking your kitten home

A conscientious breeder does not let his or her kittens go to a new owner before the age of twelve or thirteen weeks. Many breeders will bring the kitten to your home themselves. It gives them a chance to see where their carefully bred and reared kitten is going to live. Then the kitten can get quietly acquainted with its new home and companions while the person it knows is still around. The kitten's vaccination certificate will come with it. Generally the pedigree and transfer of ownership certificate will be handed over at the same time, but they may

A kitten should not leave home before the age of twelve weeks.

follow a little later. Some breeders have a sales agreement specifying the rights and obligations of both the breeder and the kitten's new owner. Make sure that you consider the contents reasonable before you sign.

Two British Shorthair parents will sometimes produce a long-haired kitten.

Kittens ought to be reared in the house.

5 THE LITTER TRAY AND TOILET TRAINING

Different kinds of cat litter

There are various different kinds of cat litter, each with its advantages and disadvantages. One of the most economical in use is clumping litter, available in either fine or coarse granules. With litter of this kind the urine does not seep through to the bottom of the tray, but binds the granules into clumps which can be easily removed. The rest of the litter remains clean. A good strong litter scoop with wide perforations is the easiest way to lift the clumps out. It is important to put a generous layer of clumping litter in the tray to prevent the urine reaching the bottom, where it is more difficult to remove. If you use litter of this kind you should remove the clumps from the tray daily. With other kinds of granular litter the urine sinks to the bottom and is partially absorbed by the porous surface of the

Dirty habits can be caused by stress.

granules. This type is cheaper but you need to use more of it, so it may ultimately be more expensive. Cheaper litters also mean more work and more cleaning. Cat litters made from wood and paper are environmentally friendly and, provided you extract solid waste, can end up as compost in the garden, but they too are often not very economical, and do not always absorb moisture and odor well.

The latest cat litters consist of synthetic globules which absorb urine and odor. You do not have to clean out the litter tray so often, and the odor is usually minimized. The cat litter you choose will depend partly on what the cat was used to with its breeder, partly on your personal preference.

Litter tray hygiene
Whichever type of litter you use, and regardless of how many cats use the tray, solid matter must be removed *at least* once a day. A litter tray is a breeding ground for bacteria, especially in summer. Not cleaning the tray thoroughly or in good time can therefore cause persistent infection in your cat or cats, and also plays a major part in the transfer of diseases. It is sensible, therefore, to empty the tray entirely once a week or once every two weeks and disinfect it, preferably with an effective disinfectant such as chlorine.

Litter trays
There are many different kinds of litter trays on the market, and they vary a good deal in both price and performance. The cheapest are open litter trays, but they are not always practical.

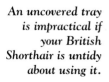

An uncovered tray is impractical if your British Shorthair is untidy about using it.

A cat will instinctively scratch over its urine and feces, and as it covers them up some of the litter can be kicked out of the tray. Some "careless" users of the litter tray will go and sit in the tray as they should but regularly deposit their feces over the edge. A tray with a cover prevents this. Since your British Shorthair, especially if he is a male, can grow into a large cat, it is best to buy as big a litter tray as possible.

Toilet training

As soon as the kittens begin eating solid food the mother cat stops cleaning them up. Either of their own accord, or with the encouragement of the mother cat or the breeder, the kittens will go in search of a litter tray. When you take a kitten into your house the little creature will thus have been house-trained for several weeks. It is sensible to start by buying the same cat litter as it was used to with its breeder. The kitten will recognise the consistency and smell of the litter, and will use the tray

Sit your kitten on the litter tray as soon as you get it home, so that it will know where to find it.

in your own house too. It is a good idea to put the kitten in the litter tray as soon as you have brought it home, so that he or she knows where to find it. If you want to change to another kind of litter at a later date you can put a little of the old, used litter on top of the new litter in the tray; the kitten will recognise the smell and will get the right idea.

Preventing dirty habits.

Cats are creatures of habit, and can become greatly attached to a certain kind or a certain brand of cat litter. If the owner then buys another kind, it can be sufficient inducement for a fastidious cat to look elsewhere for a corner to use as a loo. Moving the cat tray to a different place, or buying a different kind of litter tray, can also cause the sudden onset of dirty habits.
A litter tray is sometimes located too close to the cat's food

bowl. Putting the cat loo here may be handy for the owner, but the cat will usually find it very offensive to be expected to use the tray so close to its food, and will look for somewhere else to relieve itself. Usually, however, it is when a cat thinks the litter tray is not clean enough that he or she urinates somewhere inappropriate.

 Some cats do not like performing in a tray which has just been used by another cat. In that case, if you have several cats it is advisable to put down a separate tray for each, preferably not all in the same room but distributed around the house. There is then less likelihood of "accidents" because a cat cannot get to the tray in time, for instance when it is a long way off on the top floor, and in addition the cats like to choose their own trays.

The hormones will develop at a certain time in entire males, and they then begin spraying.

Dirty habits for hormonal reasons

British Shorthair males reach sexual maturity between the ages of seven months and a year and a half. They can then begin spraying. Spraying cats urinate not squatting but standing, quivering their tails, and the scent signal is directed not down to the floor but at a vertical surface. Entire males spray both indoors and out of doors, and although spraying is often regarded as dirty behavior it has nothing to do with dirty habits in general. It is the cat's way of asserting himself and marking out his territory. The age at which an entire male cat starts spraying and the frequency with which he does it depend very much on the individual himself. Some entire males never spray, some spray a great deal (particularly in the spring, and less or not at all during the rest of the year), and some spray only when there is a queen on call in the vicinity. Unfortunately, the various substances you can use on surfaces to deter spraying do not work with all entire males. Since almost all male cats do spray, most of them are neutered in good time. Neutering usually prevents spraying, or stops it if it had begun, but males who had been spraying for some time while they were still entire sometimes continue spraying out of habit. It is not until about six weeks after the operation that all the hormones causing a cat to spray are out of the body, so spraying will not always stop immediately after neutering.

A mother cat and her own mother looking after a litter of kittens together.

Dirty habits caused by stress and anxiety

Changes in your family, moving house, even the acquisition of a new piece of furniture can be very stressful for some cats and give rise – often only temporarily – to dirty habits. When a cat urinates or defecates on the doormat, there is a strong chance that there is a new cat in the neighborhood, either male or female, which is making your own pet feel uncomfortable and insecure. Urine and/or feces deposited on the doormat or in some other strategic place then acts as a kind of "barrier" against the neighboring cat. People in multi-cat households may find that one cat is always being persecuted by the others. This sometimes causes so much stress that the persecuted cat urinates in places away from the litter tray. It may help to spray these places with a substance containing pheromones or tracelin, but success is not guaranteed.

Other solutions to the problem of dirty habits

If the reasons for dirty habits discussed above do not apply in your case, but your cat still urinates outside the tray, it can sometimes be helpful to let your British Shorthair go out of doors. Many indoor cats stop their dirty habits when they have a chance of enlarging their territory. But there is always a chance that the cat may be a nuisance to your neighbors, and run risks itself at the same time. In most cases this means that the garden or balcony must be well fenced, and for preference made secure against attempts to escape by means of a wire with a weak electric shock, or by being roofed in. If the cat roams entirely at liberty, make sure that your pet can be identified by a microchip which a veterinarian will fit under the skin. The owner can then always be traced if the animal runs away, gets lost, and is then found. If none of these methods work, it does not necessarily mean that the cat is naturally dirty. It is possible that it and its owners, or it and any other cats or dogs in the household, simply do not click. A cat does not always express such feelings by acting in an unhappy, anxious, or aggressive way; it sometimes just develops dirty habits. Dirty cats often relieve themselves perfectly correctly in the litter tray as soon as they are in other surroundings, with another owner, and in another household. For both cat and owner, rehoming with someone you can really trust is then the only remaining solution.

When a usually clean cat develops dirty habits for no obvious reason, you should get in touch with your veterinary surgeon. There is a strong chance that the cat may have a health problem, such as diabetes (in old age), kidney problems, or inflammation of the bladder.

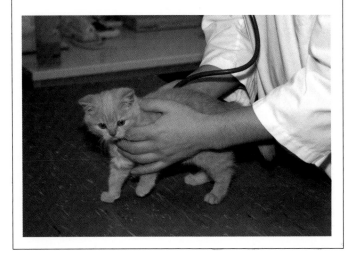

P. 45:
A five-month-old
British Shorthair
cream and white
Harlequin

6 YOUR CAT'S DIET

Cooked at home or ready-prepared?

If you are going to prepare your cat's food yourself you should know that a cat must not only get *enough* food, the *proportions* must be correctly adjusted. Getting the proportions of the nutrients wrong can ultimately cause health problems and shorten the life of your cat. If you are going to do it yourself, long and intensive study is necessary first, so most people choose to feed their cats a ready-prepared diet. Many commercial canned and dried foods of guaranteed good quality have been developed over the years, and if you choose one of those brands you will know for sure that your cat is getting all it needs.

Cheap food costs more in the long run

Cats need a diet in which the main ingredients are animal proteins and fats. Their food must consist of plenty of meat, fish, and so on. Manufacturers of good premium brands know this, and guarantee that their products contain such ingredients. Cat food of this kind is usually on the expensive side, for a very good reason: animal proteins cost more than vegetable produce. You will always pay more for a pound of rump steak than a pound of oats, and cat food manufacturers have to take that into account. As a result, it is almost impossible to manufacture cheap cat food containing enough high-quality animal fats and proteins. If you do not want to short-change your cat, you should choose the more expensive canned or dried foods.

British Shorthairs are always happy to get something nice to eat.

P. 47:
British Shorthair
*cats have a tendency to put on weight
– sometimes too
much of it.*

Extras

You can supplement the ready-prepared cat food now and then by giving your cat some extras in the form of cat treats and fresh meat, poultry, game, or fish. Any meats that could be risky to eat raw (for instance chicken, offal, and pork) must be cooked first. Other varieties, such as red meat and game, can be fed to the cat raw. Of course you will ensure that you observe the same rules of hygiene as you would when serving food to humans. If you want to give your cat milk occasionally, do not let it have cow's milk, which contains lactose and gives most cats diarrhea. Choose a milk drink specially made for cats, or kitten milk bought in powdered form to be diluted with water. Sterilized whipping cream and sterilized full-cream milk for coffee are also suitable. The lactose in cream of this kind has been made harmless by heating during the manufacturing process.

Good for the teeth

When a cat eats a natural diet of prey animals, its teeth and gums are naturally massaged and kept clean naturally. However, most cats eat their "prey" in the form of dry cat foods, ground meat or fish, and canned foods. This means that the cat has nothing which needs much chewing, so it is not surprising that cats often suffer from dental problems. To prevent them, you should regularly give your cat some food which has to be well chewed, for instance a piece of sheep's heart, a day-old chick, or dried fish. It is better to avoid feeding the cat anything containing bones, which can splinter and cause problems in the digestive system, and which can also get stuck in the mouth.

Eating grass

Cats have small barbed hooks on their tongues which help them to swallow all the hairs they lick off their coats during their daily grooming. These hairs form into a hairball in the

*Eating grass helps
a cat to bring up
a hairball more
easily.*

A self-feeding device is handy, but may encourage male neuters to eat more than they really need.

Plastic food bowls are more practical, hygienic, and durable than stainless steel dishes.

cat's stomach, and the hairball has to be brought up again. Eating grass facilitates this process. If your cat does not roam at liberty out of doors, make sure that it always has grass available, for instance the cat grass you can buy in specialist pet-care stores. If the cat has no grass available it may nibble houseplants, some of which can be poisonous.

Too fat?

British Shorthairs are attractive, cobby cats. Everything about them is rounded and substantial. But neutered and spayed cats in particular have a tendency to put on excess weight, and may develop an unattractive pot-belly. Cats who are too fat may look cosy, but being overweight is no fun for the animals themselves. As they are not feeling particularly well they take less exercise, which makes them even fatter. The overweight cat may then eat even more out of boredom, so that it is finally trapped in a downward spiral making it fatter and fatter. Being overweight places too great a burden on the cat's organs and joints. The vital organs – the heart, kidneys, and liver – are particularly vulnerable, and your cat could die prematurely.

Most adult British Shorthairs are not naturally the most active of cats, so it is a good idea to stimulate your cat to take exercise by playing with him. In that way you will keep him in good condition and prevent him from becoming overweight.

A cat who is too fat should never be simply kept on a strict diet. Cats are physiologically distinct from human beings and animals such as dogs. If an overweight cat is given nothing at all to eat for one or more days, substances which can poison it are freed in its body. The way to persuade your cat to slim is therefore never to withhold food. Instead, the cat must be stimulated to take exercise, and you should also give special diet food daily at fixed times. It is a good idea to discuss a suitable diet food for your cat with your veterinarian.

Play is essential to keep a cat in good condition.

P. 51:
The thick coat of
a British Shorthair
is excellent protec-
tion against cold.

7 CARE OF THE CAT

Care of the claws

In principle, a cat's claws never need clipping. However, the tips of the claws may sometimes still protrude even when the cat has its claws retracted, and you will then hear a clicking sound as it walks across a smooth surface. In such cases the claws may be clipped now and then. Otherwise clipping the tips of the claws is necessary only to keep your cat from injuring people or other animals, or if it is scratching the furniture a great deal. It is quite usual, for instance, to clip the tips of the claws when the cat is going to a show or before a mating. Always use good, sharp clippers made specially for the purpose, and clip only a millimeter or so off the claw, making sure that you do not cut into the quick. If you clip the tip of a kitten's claw

A good pair of clippers for your cat's claws is well worth the money.

now and then in play, the animal will be used to the experience, and you will not have to engage in a wrestling match when your cat is larger and much stronger.

The need to scratch

Every cat has a strong need to scratch, and if it lacks suitable opportunities your cat will commandeer doorposts, the wallpaper, and the furniture as substitutes for a scratching post. Once a cat has formed this habit it is a difficult one to break. So get a sturdy scratching post which will not fall over every time your cat attacks it vigorously, ensuring that it is tall

Cats have a strong urge to scratch, so a scratching post is a must for your pet.

enough for the cat to be able to have a good scratch while standing on its hind legs. Coconut matting is often used for the same purpose, and can be mounted on a vertical surface if you like.

Care of the ears
British Shorthairs have small ears with rounded tips. Owners who take their British Shorthairs to shows clip or pluck any hairs protruding above the edges and tips of the ears to accentuate the shape. Clean the ears only when necessary, using an ear-cleaner specially for cats. You can trickle the product into the auditory canal and gently work it in, and then remove the dirt that comes away from the visible part of the ear with a tissue or a cotton bud. Never insert cotton buds into the auditory canal itself, since you will only push the dirt further in, and the result may be dangerous inflammation in the inner part of the canal.

Hairs protruding above the tips of the ears are usually clipped or plucked before a show.

If you find strong-smelling dark brown to black particles in your cat's auditory canal, it may be suffering from ear-mite infestation. Ear-mites must be treated, since other cats may become infected, and they can also cause inflammation of the ear. Your veterinary surgeon   can provide remedies for ear-mites, although treatment may take some time, and not every kind of remedy is equally effective. As in so many other cases, if you accustom your kitten to having its ears cleaned while it is young, there will be few problems later.

Care of the eyes

The eyes of a British Shorthair do not generally need much care. When an otherwise healthy British Shorthair suffers from runny eyes it may sometimes have absent or malformed tear-ducts. This characteristic is inherited from Persians, some of which have to cope with the same problem. In such cases it may be necessary to consult a veterinarian and have the tear-ducts rinsed. Otherwise, all that is necessary is to remove any dirt from the corners of the eyes carefully with a tissue moistened with boiled water. Always wipe towards the nose.

Care of the teeth

Cats usual lose their milk teeth between the fourth and sixth months of life, when the adult teeth come in. It is advisable to keep an eye on this process; sometimes a milk tooth stays in the jaw, causing the adult tooth below it to grow in crooked. If you are in any doubt, always consult your veterinary surgeon.
Cats can develop caries, tartar, and gingivitis, and as with human beings, these conditions can be very painful; cats show that they are in pain by being bad-tempered, rejecting dry cat food, or becoming withdrawn. This often happens so gradually that the owner has no idea the cat is suffering. Untreated dental problems can lead to tooth loss, not to mention the pain the cat suffers from chronic inflammation. Get into the habit of

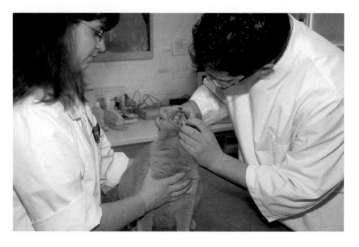

You should examine the cat's teeth regularly, or ask your veterinary surgeon to look at them.

examining the cat's teeth carefully once a month, and when you take it to the veterinarian for its annual booster vaccinations ask him or her to look at the jaw as well. Sometimes the veterinarian will have to remove tartar from an affected tooth. Try to prevent the formation of tartar by regularly giving your cat something to eat which is really hard work for the teeth (see Chapter 6: Good for the teeth, p. 46).

Care of the coat

The coat of the British Shorthair needs relatively little grooming. Brushing once a week with a bristle brush is normally enough to keep it in good condition. During the moulting seasons in spring and autumn, a small rubber brush is ideal for removing dead and loose hairs. However, do not groom too vigorously or you may damage the coat. If you regularly take your cat to shows, it is important for the coat to look good at all times. Then, during moulting, you can carefully pluck out loose hairs or those about to come away with your thumb and forefinger. This is very labor-intensive, but it prevents the coat from looking untidy.

Care of the coat is not difficult, but must be done now and then to prevent it from felting up.

Hairballs

Good care of the coat, especially in the moulting season, will prevent the cat from swallowing an unnecessarily large number of hairs which then form a hairball. In a very few cases, the cat may need an operation to remove it. Special cat foods are now available to help hairballs pass through the intestines instead of having to be vomited up.

As they wash themselves, cats swallow hairs which accumulate in the stomach.

Bathing your cat

If you show your British Shorthair, a bath is sometimes necessary. If possible choose a shampoo which suits your cat's coat color; there are shampoos which, for instance, make the coat look a clearer white or deeper black. Bath the cat at least three or four days before a show so that the coat has a chance to recover its normal condition. If you get a kitten used to being bathed while it is young, introducing it to the process as a game, there are seldom any problems when it grows up.

However, some cats hate being bathed. In that case you can work bran, non-greasy talcum power, or a dry shampoo for cats into the coat against the lie of the hairs, and then just brush it out thoroughly later. It will absorb grease and dirt, leaving the coat clean and springy.

The tail

If you are showing your British Shorthair and the tip of its tail looks rather pointed, you can make it appear rounder by clipping or gently plucking any long hairs protruding from the end. Entire males have a sebaceous gland on the dorsal surface of the tail, close to the root, which can work overtime when the animal becomes sexually mature. It produces a dark, sticky discharge of sebum which not only looks unattractive but can also

*Stud tail is a prob-
lem which regular-
ly affects entire
(stud) males.*

clog the pores of the skin, causing tufts of hair to fall out. In the
long term this condition, known as stud tail, can be treated and
to some extent prevented if you give the cat extra vitamin
B and food with a high fat content, in addition to regular appli-
cations of homeopathic calendula ointment to the affected
area. For quick results, stud tail can be treated with a dry shampoo for cats or by rubbing in cornflour. Leave the product on
the tail overnight and brush it well out again next morning.
Washing with degreasing products will give an immediate
result, but often only in the short term, since such methods
often just activate the gland more vigorously. Neutering solves
the problem permanently.

Flea control

Even cats who never go out of doors can suffer from fleas, since
you or visitors to your home can bring them in with you. You
can tell if your cat has fleas by checking the places where the
insects like to congregate, for instance the root of the tail and
along the back. Look for small brownish-black flecks. These are
the fleas' excrement, known as flea dirts. Fleas multiply very
fast indeed, and it is only a matter of weeks before just a few
fleas in your home become a positive plague.

There are many different anti-flea treatments on sale, some of
which, to be frank, are ineffective, while others work very well.
When you are buying a flea control treatment take note of the
active ingredient, and if it does not work well enough then get
a treatment based on a different ingredient next time. Besides
direct-acting insecticides in sprays, powders, and flea collars,
there are methods which take effect over a longer period,
including preparations which make a flea infertile when it has
fed on your cat's blood. You must still back these preparations

up with "conventional" methods, however, because the active
ingredient in them does not actually kills the fleas, but merely
prevents them from breeding. Treat not only the cat itself but

any other domestic pets you may have, and remember to treat the cat's environment with a spray for carpets and soft furnishings too. More than ninety percent of fleas live not on the cat itself but in its immediate surroundings, as eggs, pupae, and larvae.

Flea control for kittens is not so easy, since ant-flea treatments are aggressive and not without their risks. Always consult a veterinary surgeon. If your cat does have fleas, incidentally, you should also worm it, since fleas can carry tapeworms.

Worming

Almost all kittens have roundworms, whether or not their mother is frequently wormed. When worms are allowed to reproduce they can harm your cat's body. Kittens get their first worming while they are still with the breeder. Since worming treatments do not work on the eggs, treatment must be regular while the animal is young in order to prevent persistent infection. From one year old, it is usually sufficient to give the cat worming tablets or a worming paste once every six months. Pastes or granules are often more easily accepted by cats than tablets, which must often be forcibly administered. Some cats even seem to like the flavor of these pastes.

Kittens are nearly always infected with ringworm by their mother, even if she has been wormed herself.

Ringworm

All cat-lovers dread the fungal disease ringworm. A cat affected by ringworm may itch, and the coat will become thinner,

with bare patches. Ringworm is not life-threatening, but is highly contagious and very difficult to eradicate. The owner of a cat with ringworm can carry the spores of the fungus from place to place and thus infect other cats. Stroking a cat suffering from ringworm in the street is enough to introduce ringworm into your own home and other people's households. Cat-lovers fear ringworm so much because treatment takes a long time, and is expensive and labor-intensive.

Not only the cat (or cats) but the whole house must be treated with special products. The replacement of floor coverings and other soft furnishings in the house (curtains, sofas, bedclothes) which cannot easily be treated is often recommended. Throughout the whole period in which attempts are being made to eradicate ringworm (it can take a year or longer) it is inadvisable to visit people with cats or ask them to your house, because of the risk of transferring the infection. Fortunately veterinary science does not stand still, and a new generation of ringworm treatments based on the ingredient lufenuron is expected to come on the market soon.

Fertility

A British Shorthair female can have her first call at the age of six to fourteen months. During the call she will be more affectionate than usual, making more noise, and sticking her rear end up in the air when you stroke her back. She often drums her back paws on the ground at the same time. A calling queen will also let herself "fall over," and then lies rolling about the floor. Calling queens are not in this state all day; in between bouts of calling they will sleep a good deal, and do not look as if they were on call at all – but you can be sure that they are.

The frequency, strength, and duration of calling varies from queen to queen. Some queens are very obvious about it and make a lot of noise; in others the signs are barely noticeable.

The frequency of calling varies from queen to queen.

Some will call almost every month, others only twice a year or so. Most queens will stay on call for about five days. Calling is often triggered by warm weather, an increasing number of hours of daylight, and the presence of an entire, sexually mature male cat.

Birth control for queens

If you are not planning to let your queen have a litter of kittens, it is best to have her spayed. Then she will not come on call any more, and she will be unable to have kittens. But spaying, also known as sterilisation, is irreversible, and if you have not yet made up your mind about letting your cat have a litter some time, you can suppress calling temporarily by giving her the feline birth-control pill. If your cat seldom calls, the pill may not be necessary; you can then just let her go through the call in the usual way, although you must take extra care not to let her get out of the house while she is sexually receptive.

It is not advisable to give a queen the pill over a long period. It increases the chance of inflammation of the uterus, and can cause tumors of the lactary glands in later life. Allowing a queen to keep calling without being mated can have the same undesirable side effects. For the sake of her health, she ought to have her first litter well before her second birthday. The chance of complications increases greatly after that, so do not put off spaying any longer than necessary.

Birth control for males

Most British Shorthair males begin "spraying" – marking their territory with strong-smelling urine – between seven and fourteen months of age. Since almost all entire males spray, and their urine has a very strong odor, males to be kept as pets are often neutered before their first birthday. After neutering, spraying does not usually develop, or stops if it has started. In addition, a neutered male will no longer feel the urge to go out in search of calling queens or get into fights with potential rivals, thus running the risk of coming home with an incurable and perhaps ultimately fatal disease such as feline AIDS or feline leukemia.

If a male is neutered at the right time he will no longer have the urge to roam.

8 SICKNESS AND ABNOR- MALITIES

Symptoms of sickness

Of course it is to be hoped that your cat will not fall sick. If your kitten has come from a good breeder, and you care for it properly and provide it with a varied diet, all will usually be well. But even when every care has been taken, things can still sometimes go wrong. It is not within the scope of this book to give a full account of all possible feline complaints, but the following list of symptoms may be useful if you are worried about

---

Tekenen van ziekte
- Symptoms of sickness
- Diarrhea (not in all cases)
- Difficulty in urinating and defecating
- Faeces or urine of abnormal color
- Urinating a great deal
- Third eyelid visible
- Discharge from nose and eyes, and in queens from the vulva
- High temperature
- Dirty habits suddenly developing for no obvious reason
- Loss of appetite (the cat eats less or not at all, drinks more)
- Unusual conduct (the cat is very quiet, withdrawn, or timid)
- Skin rash
- Sudden hair loss or bare patches
- Dribbling
- Lack of interest in grooming
- Thinness
- Generally poor condition
- Bloated stomach
- Difficulty in walking
- Symptoms of paralysis
- Frequent vomiting of food (not to be confused with bringing up hairballs)

---

your cat's health. It is not comprehensive; if in any doubt, always get in touch with your veterinary surgeon.

Diarrhea

There can be many causes of diarrhea. Cats have a rather sensitive gastric and intestinal system, and in addition they are

Don't wait until your cat is really ill. Contact your vet immediatelly.

The body temperature of a cat is normally around 38.6 °C. The most reliable way of taking the temperature is anally, using a digital thermometer.

susceptible to intestinal parasites. It is important for a cat to be given high-quality food and to be regularly wormed, and hygiene must be scrupulously observed in its diet and the litter tray. Perishable food must be removed when the cat has finished feeding. In the summer months in particular, food which has been standing around for too long can cause problems. A cat with diarrhea will quickly become dehydrated, and may

Five-week-old blue kitten

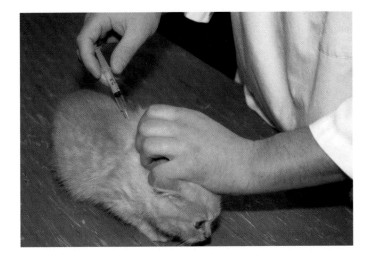

fall seriously ill or even die from lack of water. If your cat is suffering from diarrhea, do not wait too long before going to the veterinary surgeon for advice. When diarrhea keeps recurring, a bacterial culture will show what kind of medication is necessary.

Panleucopenia and feline upper respiratory disease

In their first eight weeks, kittens get antibodies to protect them against certain diseases from their mother's milk. As soon as they are eating mainly solid food, the effect of this protection begins to wear off, and it is time to have the kittens inoculated against panleucopenia and feline upper respiratory disease, highly infectious viral sicknesses which often cause death. Kittens have their first injections at the age of about eight weeks, with a second injection when they are about twelve weeks old. Inoculation against panleucopenia gives full protection; a cat with this inoculation cannot catch the disease. Even if your cat is inoculated against feline upper respiratory disease, however, he or she can still catch it, but the symptoms are much milder in an inoculated cat.

HCM (hypertrophic cardiomyopathy)

HCM is a hereditary heart disease in which the muscle of the left auricle of the heart becomes thickened and enlarged. The heart can no longer function normally. It is a common cardiac problem in cats in general, and therefore occurs in British Shorthairs. Problems often set in just when the cat is fully grown. The early symptoms are slight and can easily be overlooked; a cat appears healthy, but can suddenly fall sick or even die. Sometimes there is paralysis of the legs, a rapid heartbeat, or a heart murmur. Some cats develop only mild complaints, and seem able to go on living with them to a good age without any problems, while others die young. So far the only way of

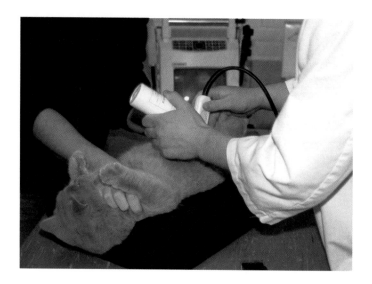

An ultrasound examination can show whether your cat is suffering from PKD.

making a diagnosis is by ultrasound, which must be carried out by a veterinary specialist with experience of the procedure, and using advanced ultrasound apparatus. There can also be other causes for thickening of the wall of the heart, so a wrong diagnosis of HCM is sometimes made. There is no cure for the complaint, but if it is diagnosed in good time specific medication can be given to provide some improvement of cardiac function.

PKD (polycystic kidney disease)

PKD is a hereditary kidney disease which occurs in other animals and human beings as well as cats. The disease is characterised by the presence of cysts (cavities filled with fluid) in both the animal's kidneys. These cysts impair kidney function, and can then lead to death. There is no cure for PKD, but the life of an affected animal can sometimes be prolonged by the right medication. Symptoms often consist of the cat's drinking and urinating a great deal. PKD occurs with various degrees of severity. An animal can die of the disease very young, or not until later life. In such cases it is often thought that the cat died of "kidney failure," but in fact it has sometimes had a mild form of PKD which finally proved fatal.

Because of the hereditary nature of PKD it is important to trace this abnormality, even though cats who have the disease can sometimes live into old age with it. Animals who do not at first sight suffer from PKD, but are in fact affected, can produce kittens who will have problems while young and die early. The diagnosis of PKD is made by ultrasound, carried out by a specialist veterinary surgeon.

Feline AIDS (FIV)

Feline AIDS, officially known as feline immunodeficiency virus (FIV), has many similarities with human AIDS.

However, it is absolutely certain that feline AIDS cannot affect humans, and vice versa. Cats can catch the virus when they are bitten by an infected cat. The cat often appears to belong to the high-risk group of entire males, roaming at liberty, who defend the borders of their territory fiercely. The chance of the virus being passed on via sexual contact is almost zero, but a positive male can pass it on to a queen through the neck-bite which is part of mating. Similarly, an infected mother cat can pass it on to her kittens during fierce play. There is no cure for FIV; although theoretically it is possible to give your cat combination therapy with advanced medication, such treatment is still in the early stages of development. There is not really any drug to combat the illness, and no inoculation which can be given to cats to protect them: an infected cat will always be a carrier of the virus, and can pass it on to other cats. A cat infected with FIV should not be allowed to come into contact with other cats, although there will always be the risk of its biting another cat.

The only way of ensuring that your cat does not contract the virus is not to let it come into contact with any animals which may be affected. This means never letting your cat roam free out of doors. Do not forget to have the cats already in your household and any new arrivals tested, especially if they have ever been strays or rescue cats in the past.

The insidious nature of FIV lies in the different course that the sickness can take. Some cats fall sick very soon after becoming affected; others do not show symptoms until some time later – as much as up to five years after infection – and some cats grow to a reasonably old age with it. Symptoms which may occur include high temperature, diarrhea, character change, persistent inflammations (especially of the gums), anemia, persistent feline respiratory disease, enlarged lymph nodes, unusual cancerous tumors, and weight loss. To find out whether a cat has FIV you can have its blood tested for the presence of antibod-

A cat who roams freely out of doors can come into contact with two viral diseases: AIDS and feline leukaemia.

ies against the virus. Cat breeders always test their breeding stock for the presence of antibodies in the blood, so you can be sure of obtaining an AIDS-free kitten from them.

Infectious leukemia (FeLV)

Infectious leukemia, officially called feline leukaemia virus (FeLV), is a virus sickness which can affect cats of any age. Cats can catch the virus when they are bitten by an infected animal, but also, to a lesser extent, by eating with such an animal, washing each other's coats, or sharing a litter tray. Because the virus attacks the cat's immune system, the symptoms can vary. The cat can, for instance, be more vulnerable to all kinds of viruses and bacteria. In addition, the virus can be the cause of tumors in the lymph glands and other organs.

Infectious leukemia is incurable. An inoculation against it is available, but its use is not yet universal world-wide, since some owners do not believe that it provides complete protection. Although in the United Kingdom breeders accept it as standard, many breeders in other countries opt instead to have a blood test done on their animals which will show the presence of antibodies against FeLV. If there is any infection near

Eye color
The eye color of British Shorthairs becomes less intense with age. The process is not always a gradual one. A fleck of the old color can remain in the eye, and is not a sign of sickness.

The ideal cat carrier opens at the top.

your house do not let your cat roam out of doors where it could be infected, and always have the blood of your existing cats and any newcomers tested for the presence of antibodies.

Patellar luxation (PL)

Patellar luxation (PL) is a hereditary deformity of the knees

Blue-cream queen with her three kittens

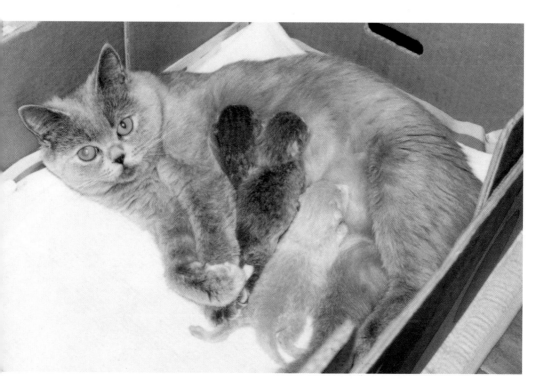

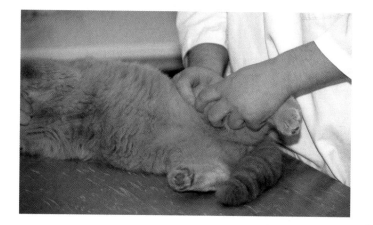

The presence or absence of patellar luxation can be established by handling.

sometimes found in various breeds of cats and dogs, including the British Shorthair. The characteristic feature of the deformity is that the knee joints are displaced to a greater or lesser extent. In the worst case, they can become displaced at the slightest movement, which makes bending and therefore normal walking or jumping impossible. In easily the majority of cases, however, the patellar luxation is only slight, and the cat experiences relatively little disability. A diagnosis can be made by a good veterinary surgeon, who will see how far the knee joints give under slight pressure. In cats suffering severely from PL an operation, carried out in a special animal hospital, can improve the condition.

Skeletal abnormalities

Bone abnormalities are unusual in the British Shorthair. In some breeding lines, flat-chested kittens do appear now and then. This is a hereditary condition in which the form of the ribcage is not rounded but flattened. The precise way in which it is passed on is not certain, but breeders will generally avoid using such animals in their programmes.

Small abnormalities of the tail sometimes occur, as they do in every pedigree breed and in non-pedigree cats. This is only a "fault" in relation to the cat's overall appearance, and does not affect its health. However, breeders keep a careful eye open for the condition, since a cat with a tail fault will never win the highest awards in a show.

Finally, a number of cats have recently and unintentionally been registered as British Shorthairs out of ignorance; in fact they belong to a different breed, the Scottish Fold. The mutation responsible for the folded ears in this breed can also cause malformations in other parts of the skeleton, so it is inadvisable to breed from British Shorthairs which have Scottish Folds in their ancestry.

P. 70:
Young bi-color blue and white male

P. 73:
Red without any
ghost markings is
one of the most dif-
ficult colors to
breed.

9 BREEDING BRITISH SHORTHAIRS

Points specific to breeding British Shorthairs

A whole book could be written on the subjects of feline mating, pregnancy, kittening, and the rearing of kittens alone. However, these general subjects do not come within the scope of a book on the British Shorthair, so you will find here only points to be borne in mind when you are planning to raise kittens of this specific breed.

A suitable queen?

If you are thinking of breeding a litter of kittens from your British Shorthair queen, there are a number of things which you should bear in mind. Simply breeding a litter without further thought is extremely unwise, and will serve no good purpose. A British Shorthair queen is a pedigree cat whose *raison d'être* lies in her appearance. Breeding from a pedigree cat means that you must aim to improve the breed, not just increase its num-

A silver tabby queen with her newborn kittens

bers. To find out if your queen will pass muster in the face of criticism, you could enter her in a cat show once or several times. And as it is no use to anyone to breed a litter from a queen who may pass problems on to her kittens, before you mate your queen you should have her examined by a good veterinary surgeon who has plenty of experience with pedigree cats. He or she can establish whether your cat is in good condition, if she has well-shaped tearducts, whether her knee joints are too loose (PL), and whether she has a well-formed pelvis. She can be given the two blood tests for feline leukaemia and feline AIDS at the same time. You can get a specialist to check her kidneys for the absence of hereditary cysts (PKD) and perhaps have an ultrasound examination of her heart carried out. It is important, of course, for a breeding queen to have sound cardiac and kidney functions; both of these will be required to get her safely through kittening, and help her to stand up to the considerable physical demands of pregnancy and suckling.

Blood groups
Two different blood groups occur in British Shorthairs: they inherit either the dominant blood group A or the recessive blood group b. In most breeds of cat, blood group A is predominant.
It is characteristic of British Shorthairs, however, that at least half of them have blood group b. Feline blood plasma contains antibodies against any different blood group, so the blood must not come into contact with such a group. In practice, problems arise only when a queen of blood group b is mated by a stud of blood group A. Some of the kittens will be born with blood group A, and during the first eighteen to twenty-four hours of life these kittens can take in the antibodies which are deadly to them with their mother's milk. The cause of death is FNI (feline

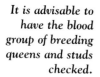

It is advisable to have the blood group of breeding queens and studs checked.

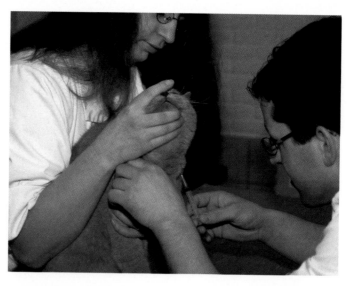

neonatal isoerythrolysis), meaning that the antibodies destroy the red blood corpuscles. Some kittens die very soon after birth, but in most cases they suckle only with difficulty or not at all, and display general weakness before dying. Reddish-brown urine is extremely typical of FNI. Some kittens miraculously survive, but they often remain weak and suffer from anemia.

Any potential problems can be anticipated by having every breeding queen's blood group determined before she has a litter. Only when a queen of blood group b is mated to a stud of blood group A will a breeder know in advance that there may be such problems. They can be countered by giving the kittens nothing but special kitten milk during the first twenty-four hours of their lives. After this initial period they can suckle from their mother, because by then the kittens' intestinal walls are no longer absorbing the antibodies. The kittens can stay close to their mother for the first twenty-four hours, but you must ensure that they drink only the substitute milk.

Left: A newborn silver tabby kitten

Right: The inherited recessive longhair gene means that two shorthaired cats can produce a longhaired kitten.

Longhaired cats

The British Shorthair is descended from robust shorthaired cats which were crossed now and then with Persians to improve the type and introduce new colors, and this practice is still very occasionally followed. A legacy from this past history, logically enough, is that some British Shorthairs carry a recessive longhair factor. As a result, longhair kittens are sometimes born to British Shorthair parents, and are generally designated British Variants. Some people would like to make such longhaired cats a separate breed, but most breeders see them as a by-product of their British Shorthair breeding, and let the kittens go to cat-lovers as pets at a lower price.

P. 77:
Blue is the dilute
form of black.

10 GENETICS

Genetics

Some knowledge of the laws of heredity, i.e. genetics, is essential for every breeder. If a breeder knows enough about the subject, he or she can apply its rules in practice, and can thus predict reasonably well what the "outcome" of a certain mating will be. For instance, a breeder who knows something about genetics and has studied the pedigrees of his or her breeding animals will not be surprised when two blue parents produce a colorpointed kitten. Such breeders also know that they need not expect a blue male kitten from the mating of a cream queen to a blue stud, and that no problems need be expected if a queen of blood group b is mated to a stud of the same blood group. Unfortunately most books on genetics are full of involved terminology, codes, and diagrams, and discourage many people in advance from wishing to immerse themselves in the subject. But the basic principles are not really as difficult as they look; anyone can master them.

Melanins

The various coat colors of cats are the result of the refraction of light on small pigment particles present in the hairs. These pigment particles can differ in shape and size, and can lie close to each other in groups or be freely and uniformly distributed in the hair shaft. The pigment particles are called melanins. All coat colors in cats are created by two basic melanins: phaeomelanin produces a red coat color, and eumelanin is responsible for a black coat. In the course of time various mutations have caused the melanins to change shape or diverge from their original positions, so that the light falls on

White spotting is
passed on by
a dominant gene.

the hairs in a different way and a different color is produced. Chocolate and cinnamon are thus mutations of black. Another mutation makes the melanins cluster together, leaving empty space between the clusters, so that the coat color is optically pale. Black (eumelanin) then appears blue, chocolate becomes lilac, and cinnamon becomes fawn. There may also be deviations from the standard form with phaeomelanin (red), but the differences in coat color are optically so indistinct that all the shades are usually just described as red. The clustering phenomenon, however, can be clearly distinguished in coats containing phaeomelanins, and in that case the red color fades to cream.

Chromosomes

Animals have a number of paired chromosomes storing genetic information in every cell of their bodies. The cat has 38 pairs of chromosomes, except in the sperm cells of males and the egg cells of females. These cells contain single chromosomes instead of pairs. This is logical, since the merging of the single chromosomes in the egg cell and the sperm cell will produce a new set of paired chromosomes. If egg cells and sperm cells contained pairs of chromosomes, then their progeny (when viable) would have not one but two pairs of chromosomes, when they were mated in their own turn their progeny would have four pairs of chromosomes, and so on. Nature has arranged things well. The division of the pairs of chromosomes, a process known as meiosis, means that in the reproductive process the number of chromosomes always remains the same. A young creature will thus always inherit half its characteristics from its father and half from its mother.

Genes

The genes are located on the pairs of chromosomes, and store all the genetic data inherited by the animal. Taken together, these genes contain all the information necessary for a new life.

Pregnant queen: her kittens will inherit half their qualities from her and the other half from their father.

Lilac is a dilute form of chocolate.

Characteristics such as the length, color, and pattern of a cat's coat, the length of its legs and shape of the ears, are determined by these genes. But characteristics which do not show on the outside are genetically determined as well, for instance susceptibility to certain abnormalities, and the working of the cat's digestive system. The genes contain only inherited material, and thus determine an animal's hereditary qualities. Genes cannot pass on characteristics acquired through external factors, such as an amputated tail.

Temperamental qualities are also inherited, but only to a certain extent. An animal may, for instance, have a hereditary tendency to be aggressive, but if it is well cared for and never gets into situations where its aggression can develop, this hereditary tendency will not be expressed, or will be kept within bounds. A susceptibility to certain illnesses can be inherited in the same way. Here, however, we will confine ourselves to the way in which colors are inherited, the subject about which most is known in the field of feline genetics.

Dominant and recessive genes

In a natural mating, an arbitrary chromosome from the male will encounter an arbitrary chromosome from the queen. The pairs of chromosomes contain two genes for each characteristic, that is to say double information. The genes do not merge. If they did, then a cross between a black cat and a white cat would produce grey kittens, which is not the case. The reason is that some genes are dominant and others recessive. Dominance means that a quality is expressed more strongly than a recessive factor, and will thus always be displayed in the outward appearance of the animal if it has inherited the dominant gene for that quality from one parent. Recessive genes will show in the outward appearance of the cat only if they are not suppressed by

Genetically, the white cat is the same color as its playmate, but because it also has the dominant W gene, the white covers the real color like a white sheet.

a dominant gene. If the animal shows a recessive quality, for instance the color chocolate, then it cannot be carrying the gene for black coat color, since in that case, as black is dominant over chocolate, the cat would have been black. A gene is almost always either dominant or recessive in relation to another gene. Exceptions are the separate phaeomelanins and eumelanins, which can show themselves side by side and, being located on the sex chromosomes, are sexually inherited.

An example

A mating between a black cat with only black ancestors and a chocolate cat will produce a litter consisting entirely of black kittens. The kittens will have inherited the dominant gene for black from one parent and the recessive gene for chocolate from the other. Kittens born from this mating will thus carry chocolate in their genetic makeup, even though it does not show. Animals of this kind are described as "carriers" of a certain quality; in this case, they carry chocolate. If a mating between a brother and sister from this litter now takes place, there is a good chance that a number of the young will receive the recessive gene for chocolate from both parents, and as a result one or more chocolate kittens will be born from the black parents. The quality present but invisible in the parent animals has been brought out when two recessive genes encountered each other. A mating between two black cats can thus produce chocolate kittens, but not the other way around. What the cat does not carry cannot be brought out, and since chocolates cannot carry the gene for black (or they would have been black themselves) two chocolates cannot produce black kittens together.

Surprises

The merging of genes is entirely arbitrary, so it may also happen, purely by chance, that no carriers of the same recessive gene are mated to each other for generations, or that when two carriers of a recessive quality do mate a dominant gene always encounters a recessive gene, preventing expression of the recessive gene in the cat's outward appearance. Theoretically, for example, two British Shorthairs, neither of which has any colorpointed ancestors in its pedigree, can produce one or more colorpointed kittens; the colorpointed pattern is inherited as a recessive gene in relation to normal coloring. Research further back into the pedigree will then show that one or more ancestors were in fact colorpointed cats, but too far back in the past to be still shown on the pedigree. Although it has taken a long time, ultimately two animals which both carry the recessive gene involved have been mated, and these genes have encountered each other in the merging of egg cell and sperm cell. The chance of this happening may be small, but such a chance can never be entirely ruled out when there are recessive genes present.

Without the double presence of the cs gene, this blue colorpointed kitten would have been blue all over.

Breeding true

Animals which we know for sure have no "surprise packets" such as those described above are said to breed true. In genetic terms, these animals are also described as homozygous for the color in question. An animal which has a recessive external characteristic is thus always homozygous for that quality. When cats show a dominant characteristic, one can never be a hundred percent sure that they are homozygous for that quality. A non-dilute color (red, black, chocolate), for instance, is always dominant in relation to a dilute color (cream, blue, lilac). A red British Shorthair which is known to have one cream parent must also carry the recessive dilute gene as well as the dominant gene for dense (non-dilute) red. Such animals are said not to breed true, and are described as heterozygous. These cats carry or can pass on the dilute color. In general a mating between a dilute cat and a carrier of the dilute color concerned is enough to produce dilute kittens, but sometimes several litters will be necessary before they appear, since the merging of genes is always arbitrary. Nevertheless, a definite pattern of inheritance has been established. This pattern holds good in principle only for large numbers, but it can be discerned even with small numbers.

Heterozygous = non-true-breeding: two different genes for a certain
                quality
Homozygous = true-breeding: two identical genes for a certain quality

"Dense color" versus "dilute color"
The colors in the column on the right are dilute versions of the colors in
the column on the left

Red   Cream
Black   Blue
Chocolate   Lilac
Cinnamon   Fawn

*Blue colorpointed
kitten*

Symbols

Dominant and recessive qualities are indicated by codes. These codes for feline genetics were scientifically established in the 1950s by an international commission headed by the British geneticist Roy Robinson. A dominant quality is always indicated by a capital letter. Taking black as an example, it is B. Each color or quality thus has its own code. Colors and patterns, such as the presence or otherwise of white spotting, silver, or colorpointed markings, are always passed on independently of each other, which means that the genetic code of a cat is longer than just two letters. Usually it is a question of a dominant version with a recessive counterpart, but sometimes there are two dominant versions which react in an intermediary way on each other, and at other times there are two or three recessive counterparts which may or may not preserve a certain hierarchy among themselves. In the box below you will find the most usual qualities and their codes.

Genetic symbols
(Dominant on the left, corresponding recessive qualities on the right)

A	Agouti	**a**	non-agouti
B	Black	**b**	chocolate / bl cinnamon
C	Complete pigmentation	**cs**	point-restricted coloring (points)
D	Dense	**d**	dilute
I	Inhibited (silver)	**i**	non-inhibited (not silver)
S	(Piebald white) Spotting	**s**	non-piebald white spotting
Sp	Spotted (spotted	**sp**	non-spotted or patched tabby pattern)
T	Mackerel (striped)/	**tb**	blotched
		Ta	Aby pattern (ticked)
W	White	**w**	non-white

Calculating the chances

Black, indicated by a capital B, is dominant as a coat color over chocolate, indicated by a small b. When a homozygous black British Shorthair (BB) is mated to a homozygous chocolate British Shorthair (bb), we can be certain that there will be a B in every sperm cell of the stud cat and a b in every egg cell of the queen. When egg cell and sperm cell merge, the genetic code for the color of the kittens' coat will thus always be Bb. The dominant coat color will show in all the kittens, and they will be black. However, they carry chocolate in their genetic make-up, even though it is invisible. If these kittens are now crossed with each other, there may be egg cells with Bs and egg cells with bs, and the stud cat too can produce sperm cells with Bs or bs. The queen's B can thus encounter the stud's B (BB),

but there is also a chance that two bs will meet (bb), or one B and one b (Bb):

BB homozygous black
Bb heterozygous black
bb (homozygous) chocolate

The litter in this example will thus consist of black and chocolate kittens. When these genes are set out in a diagram, it becomes clear that the chance of a B encountering a b is greater than that of two Bs or two bs coming together. Seen in terms of percentages, roughly 25% of the kittens in the litter will be homozygous black (BB), another 25% will be homozygous chocolate (bb), and the chance of heterozygous black kittens (Bb) is 50%. But caution is necessary here; these percentages show clearly only in large numbers, and a single litter is not representative. Genetics help us to work out which colors definitely can *not* be produced by a certain mating, and to calculate the chances of the colors which *may* be produced by it. However, we can never predict exactly which colors will

P. 87:
Lilac-cream queen

be born – within the limits of the genetic possibilities, that is – or how many kittens will be of a given color. Only the *chances* can be calculated.

Inheritance of red and black in male cats

The main coat colors in the cat – red and black, and derivatives of those colors – are not passed on through dominance or recession, but are sex-linked. To understand how they are

Diagram		
	B	b
B	BB	Bb
b	Bb	bb

inherited, you first need to know that females have two X chromosomes (XX) and males have one X chromosome and one Y chromosome (YX). Since all pairs of chromosomes divide in the formation of egg and sperm cells, the queen's egg cells can contain only X chromosomes, while the male's sperm cells can contain an X or Y chromosome. The genes determining the color of the cat are located only on X chromosomes. Y chromosomes are thus "idle" where color is concerned, and we have to look only at the X chromosomes to see how red and black are inherited. The two kinds of melanins cannot occur side by

Males can inherit their color only from their mothers: the cream kittens in this litter are thus male.

White patches are a random inheritance; the pattern of the markings cannot be predicted.

Tortoise shell males

Now and then a tortie male is born: a male kitten with both eumelanin and phaeomelanin in his coat. Such a male has a Y chromosome and not one but two X chromosomes, and is usually sterile. If a tortie male actually is fertile, another phenomenon called a chimera is involved. It can happen occasionally that two clusters of cells merge at an early embryonic stage, and one kitten instead of two develops. A (possibly tortie) male resulting from such a merging of cells is fertile, and in certain parts of his body can exhibit different DNA.

Samson, a tortoise shell male who created a sensation at English cat shows around 1900.

side on a single X chromosome. The gene contains either a eumelanin or a phaeomelanin. The genetic symbol for phaeomelanin (red, with its dilute version cream) is O, and the symbol for eumelanin (black with its derivative versions chocolate and cinnamon) is o. It follows that male cats can get their color only from their mother: they have taken the X gene from her, and the "colorless" Y gene which makes them male from their father. If the mother cat is black (XoXo), then all the males in her litter will be black (YXo). If the mother cat is red (XOXO) then all the males in her litter will be red (YXO). If she is tortoiseshell (XOXo), then her sons can be either black (YXo) or red (YXO). The chances of black or red kittens from a tortie mother are random, but in theory they are equal at 50%.

Inheritance of red and black in female cats

The color of the male influences only the female member of his progeny. They have two X chromosomes; one from their mother and one from their father. The color of the female kittens is thus determined by both the sire and dam. If the mother is black (XoXo) and the father red (YXO), then the dam can pass on only black (Xo) and the sire red (XO) to the daughters. The two melanins are not dominant or recessive in respect of each other, and can thus both show in the outward appearance of the female kittens. A queen receiving this combination has the genetic code XOXo, and as a result is a tortoiseshell, or tortie for short. A tortie (XOXo) mated to a black male (YXo) can have both female torties (XOXo) and female black kittens (XoXo). Mated to a red male (YXO) the possible combinations are XOXO and XOXo, i.e. red and tortie females respectively. At the same time, this explains why two black cats can never have red or tortie kittens, and two red cats can never produce black kittens

Blue-cream queen. The convergence of eumelanins and phaeomelanins appears only in female cats.

A blotched blue tabby queen. The blotched tabby pattern is passed on as recessive to other tabby patterns.

Genetics in practice

The range of possible colors is enormous, and the same, of course, is true of other characteristics. Unfortunately they are not all passed on with the elegant simplicity of the dominant or recessive effect, or as independently of each other as the examples of coat colors and markings given above. Some qualities come to light only when another gene is present to activate the operation of certain genes. This, for instance, is the case with tabbies. All cats, regardless of color, have double tabby genes and thus a tabby pattern. Unless the dominant agouti gene is inherited, however, these tabby genes can never show in the cat's outward appearance.

There are also some genes which go together with other genes. The colorpointed pattern, for example, is indissolubly linked to blue eyes, and a breeder can never raise colorpointed cats with orange eyes. In addition, many qualities are inherited polygenetically, for instance the size of the ears, the precise shade of the main coat color, or the size and shape of the individual cat. There is a great deal for a novice breeder to learn in this field. For those who are interested, it will be useful to know that many books have been published which go further into the subject of feline genetics than it has been possible to do here.

P. 91:
Many factors united in a single queen: black tortie, blotched tabby, and silver.

P. 93:
*This non-agouti
cream queen shows
no ghost markings
because she carries
the ticked tabby
pattern.*

11 SELF COLORS AND TORTIE

In general

The British Shorthair is bred in all the self (or solid) colors. There should be no tabby markings and, with the exception of the Self White BSH, no white hairs in the coats of self-colored British Shorthairs. Each hair must as far as possible be of the same color all the way down; as the breed standard puts it, "of a single color, sound to the roots." Self-colored kittens usually have the faint tabby pattern known as ghost marking in their coats while they are young. This ghost marking will usually fade when the animal is older, and within a year there is usually no sign of it left. Sometimes these faint tabby markings do happen to remain partly visible in an adult animal, especially on the tail and sometimes the legs. In adult cats, such ghost markings will be considered withholding faults at shows, although they are allowed to pass in kittens.

*Below left:
Eye color becomes
paler as the cat
ages; in this white
neuter the eyes
have turned almost
yellow.*

*Below right:
Cream male with
magnificent deep
orange eye color.*

Eye color

All self-colored British Shorthairs should have orange eyes with no green flecks or rims. The white BSH is the exception, and may have one orange and one blue eye; it is then described as odd-eyed. Young kittens always have blue eyes. When the kitten is about six weeks old the eye color begins to change, and by the time the animal is ten months old the eyes have taken on their adult color. The eye color always becomes less intensely pigmented in the older cat. Elderly orange-eyed

British Shorthairs often have golden to yellowish eyes. Some further remarks about the various self colors are given below.

Black
The coat of a black British Shorthair must be jet black, without any rusty tinge. It is in fact difficult to achieve this shade of color because black is inclined to become rather rusty under the influence of sunlight and moisture (through washing and the absorption of enzymes from the saliva). Only partners with deep orange eyes should be considered for mating with black British Shorthairs. Since a coat which is not solidly colored throughout is very conspicuous in black British Shorthairs, the partner of a black cat must have an excellent, even coat color. As far as possible every hair should be of exactly the same shade right down to the root. There is no short cut to breeding a beautiful deep black, evenly colored British Shorthair with deep orange eyes; these qualities are achieved only after a long process of consistent selection.

Blue
Blue is the dilute form of black. The term "blue" is really rather misleading: it would be better to speak of a "grey" cat. But nineteenth-century cat-lovers thought the term "blue" more elegant, and liked a shade of grey with a trace of slaty blue in it, and so the term has become firmly established in the cat world. Blue British Shorthairs have been bred since the beginning of the history of the breed, when they were extremely popular. Today blue is still one of the most sought-after colors

Blue male

Chartreux versus British Blue

British Blues are sometimes and erroneously called Chartreux cats. The Chartreux is not in fact a British Shorthair, but is recognized as a separate French cat breed. The cats are very similar, but the Chartreux has its own breed standard, which differs in several points from the British. The ears are larger, pointed, and held more erect on the head. In addition the head shape is not absolutely round but more angular, with the shape of a reverse triangle.

The Chartreux is not a British Blue but a French breed of cat.

It is difficult to breed red non-agouti cats without any ghost markings.

in the breed. The British Blue should have a light to medium blue coat, identical in tone over the whole body.

Red

Red is a phaeomelanin, and since the gene for non-agouti does not have much effect on this kind of pigmentation a tabby pattern often shows through, even when the cat is not agouti (i.e. visibly tabby). Breeding self red cats with a beautifully solid coat color is therefore a difficult task, and this is one reason why red is not a popular color with breeders. Attempts have been made in the past to get rid of the unwanted faint tabby ghost markings in these colors by selecting cats whose tabby markings were as indistinct as possible, but without success. As a result the ticked tabby gene was later bred in. The ticked tabby pattern is very much like the coat of a wild rabbit, and dispenses with the clear pattern of the striped or mackerel and blotched or classic tabbies. When ticked tabby shows through in the coat, it is hardly noticeable at all, and in this way breeders have thus succeeded in producing coats of a relatively solid red color.

Cream

Cream is the dilute version of red, but in contrast to the self red, it has proved possible over the years to breed a reasonably solid-colored cream British Shorthair – not by incrossing with the ticked tabby gene, but by decades of consistent breeding with animals showing as little as possible in the way of ghost markings. For this reason British Creams are not generally mated to tabbies – to do so would destroy, in one fell swoop, the results of a process of selection that has gone on for nearly a century. However, creams too often show remnants of the tabby pattern, although they are often visible only as rings on the tail. In order to breed out these final traces of tabby markings, some breeders are now crossing the ticked tabby pattern into creams.

Cream must be of as pale a shade as possible. Consequently, British Creams are generally mated with other dilute colors such as creams like themselves, blues, blue-creams, or lilacs. The top coat and undercoat must also be uniform in color, which is not always the case with the British Cream.

White

The gene which produces an entirely white coat is the W gene. This gene ensures that the cat looks pure white all over. Genetically, however, the cat can carry any other color and any other pattern under its white coat unseen, including white spotting, and these colors can be passed on to its progeny. In these animals the white is, as it were, a kind of sheet spread over the true color. Young kittens often have a colored spot between the ears which fades with age. This spot shows the cat's real color, still present underneath the white, and can give the breeder some indication of the possible colors which may be passed on by a cat which itself is pure white throughout its adult life. A white show cat may therefore be permitted to have a colored spot on the head as a kitten, until it is entered for adult classes at shows. Depending on the color they carry under their white coats, white British Shorthairs have orange or blue eyes, or one eye orange and one blue (odd-eyed white). They can be mated to any other colors of British Shorthairs so long as these cats too have deep orange or blue eyes. British Shorthairs with green eyes are not suitable partners, since there is then a strong chance that several kittens would be born with undesirable eye color.

The coat should be pure white, but these cats do sometimes have a hint of yellow in certain places. These marks may be caused by hormonal fluctuations, ingredients in the cat's diet,

Left:
White queen with orange eyes

Right:
This kitten still shows a spot of blue color.

or external factors such as dirt and moisture. A show cat should be bathed now and then with a special shampoo for white cats, so that it will look its best at a show.

White cats and deafness
A breeder of white British Shorthairs must be particularly careful, because the W gene which produces a pure white coat may

This blue-eyed white kitten has excellent hearing; genetically, it is colorpointed.

be linked to congenital deafness. The color of the eyes is not a factor; it is a misconception that cats with blue eyes are deaf and those with orange eyes are not. The condition can occur with both eye colors. To minimize the risk of deafness, two white cats are never mated to each other. In addition, it is wiser not to breed from cats known to have several deaf ancestors, or to have produced deaf kittens in a litter of their own. It is often difficult to detect whether a cat is deaf or not, but there is a "Baer" test which can establish whether the animal is deaf in one or both ears. Cats deaf in both ears or only one will not be used in breeding. White cats with two blue eyes were very unusual until quite recently, because the risks of producing deaf kittens dissuaded breeders from mating two white cats, and it was precisely the combination of two white parents which gave the highest chance of blue-eyed white kittens. Today, however, and with the help of blue-eyed colorpointed British Shorthairs, it is possible to breed in blue eyes under the "white coat." Such cats have normal voices and good hearing.

Tortoiseshell or tortie

Tortie British Shorthairs should have a coat with both red and black areas. The red blaze on the nose which is often present is an attractive bonus. The arrangement of eumelanins and phaeomelanins in the coat is a matter of chance, and the disposition of the colors is different in every tortie cat. At shows, however, all other things being equal, preference goes to cats with evenly intermingled colors. Tortie cats are almost always female, and are usually mated to black, red, cream, or blue British Shorthairs.

Below left:
Black tortie queen

Below right:
Chocolate

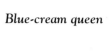

Blue-cream queen

Young lilac male

Blue-cream

Blue-cream is a dilute version of tortie. The black has "faded" to blue, and the red to cream. As light as possible a shade of both colors is preferred. In this color, preference is given to a well intermingled coat; large patches of the colors are not really desirable. However, the distribution of the colors is unpredictable and cannot be fixed. Young kittens of this color are usually predominantly blue, but as they grow up the cream comes through clearly. The correct eye color in these cats, as with all self cats, is deep copper to orange. Blue-cream queens are usually mated to blue, lilac, and cream British Shorthairs, but in principle any self color with orange eyes can be a suitable partner.

12 TABBIES

Agouti
Cats with a tabby pattern have the dominant agouti gene through which the tendency to show a certain tabby pattern is inherited. The pattern develops because to a greater or lesser extent the agouti gene suppresses the formation of the basic color in certain places. In this way alternating bands of dark and light coloring appear on each hair. The darker color of banding shows the cat's underlying color. The chin and lips of tabbies are often pale or almost white in color, but should not be really white. The nose leather is not evenly colored but has a dark outline round it.

Orange and green eyes
The eyes can be either deep orange, with no green flecks or rims, or an attractive, solid deep green. Tabbies with green eyes are known as golden tabbies, and in other respects are the same as "normal" tabbies, the only difference being the eye color. Golden tabbies are usually born of silver tabby bloodlines containing green-eyed ancestors. On principle, cats with green eyes are not mated to cats with orange eyes and vice versa, since such a cross impairs the depth of both eye colors, producing an intermediate shade which does not meet the ideal standard of either color.

Blotched or classic tabbies
Blotched tabbies are also known as classic tabbies. Cats with this pattern must have a tail with broad, regular rings, and the legs must show broad rings as well. The neck and the upper part of the chest should show unbroken necklaces. A distinct line runs over the top of the head and extends to the shoulder

Blotched (classic)
red tabby male

markings which, when viewed from above, form a butterfly pattern on each side. The central areas of the "wings" of this butterfly show small patches of the ground color. An unbroken line runs down the spine from the butterfly to the tail, and there should be a stripe either side of this spine line, running parallel to it, and separated by stripes of ground color. Another feature of the blotched or classic tabby pattern is the "oyster" patch on each flank, surrounded by one or more unbroken rings. The oyster pattern must be the same on both sides. There should also be blotches on the stomach. The forehead shows a clear "M" marking, with a stripe running back from the outer corner of the eye. The markings should be well defined and stand out clearly from the ground color. Many people regard the classic or blotched tabby as the most spectacular of all British Shorthair tabby patterns in appearance.

Mackerel or striped tabby

The striped or mackerel tabby is almost identical with the blotched tabby in respect of the tabby pattern on stomach, head, legs, and tail. Instead of the dramatic oyster and butterfly markings, however, striped tabbies should have vertical, unbroken stripes on the sides, with a dark spine line running from the back of the head to the tail. The stripes on the flanks should be as narrow and numerous as possible. The stripes on legs and tail are also finer and thinner in the striped or mackerel tabby than in the blotched, classic tabby.

Spotted tabby

The spotted tabby British Shorthair has become popular recently, particularly in the black silver coloring. The spots are caused by the dominant Sp gene, which is passed on independently of the genes producing striped or blotched patterns, and which interrupts the development of those patterns. On a spotted tabby, it is sometimes still possible to see clearly which the

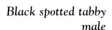
Black spotted tabby male

underlying tabby pattern is. The spotted tabby should show the same patterning on the head, legs, tail, chest, and stomach as the blotched and striped tabbies, but must have a clearly defined pattern of spots on the sides and back. This ideal can be achieved by consistently breeding from animals with as good a spotted pattern as possible.

Ticked tabby

The ticked tabby is the tabby pattern familiar to us from the Abyssinian cat, and is present in wild rabbits. A ticked tabby is really unpatterned over most of the body, but each separate hair shows agouti banding. Unlike the other tabbies, a ticked tabby does not have to have any markings on the body, although faint stripes do appear on the legs and tail. British Shorthair ticked tabbies are not widely bred, but they are used in the breeding of self red and cream British Shorthairs.

Black tabbies

Black tabbies, whatever their tabby pattern, should have as deep brown a ground color as possible. A sallow, greyish ground color is highly undesirable. The requisite deep brown is poly-genetically caused, and this warm ground color can be

Cream female,
genetically
a ticked tabby

achieved only by selection. Black tabbies are sometimes called brown tabbies, although this is really erroneous, since it refers to the ground color, while all other tabbies are named for the color of their markings (blue tabby, red tabby, lilac tabby), and ideally this confusing term would disappear from the terminology of the cat world.

Black spotted tabby male

The tabby pattern is excellent camouflage.

Black tabbies have orange eyes and can be mated to self-colored British Shorthairs with orange eyes and to orange-eyed tabbies of the same tabby pattern. Black tabbies with this eye color, however, are not widely bred at present.

One golden tabby and three silver tabby kittens in the same litter

Tortie tabbies

Tortie tabbies have coats containing both eumalanins and phaeomelanins combined with a tabby pattern; that is to say, both main colors display a pattern. Tortie tabbies occur in all the colors, both dense and dilute. It is essential for the pattern of both colors to be visible in the coat. Tortie tabbies may have either orange or green eyes.

P. 107:
Black and white
bi-color female

13 BRITISH SHORTHAIRS WITH WHITE (BI-COLORS)

White patches

Bi-colors, that is to say cats with white patches in their coats, are the result of the presence of the dominant S gene. This gene prevents the formation of pigment in certain parts of the coat. The process determining where the cat is colored and where it remains white occurs at the embryonic stage. Typically, the distribution of colored and white patches is from above to below. On top of the cat (on its back, ears, and tail) it is still colored, underneath (on the stomach, chin, and neck) it is not. The amount of white is polygenetically

Young blue and white bi-color male

the influence of the polygenes, making an excellent contrast between the pattern of the top coat and the pale ground color of the undercoat. If there are few polygenes present, cats with a poor silver undercoat are born. In silver tabbies and tipped cats, this is expressed in discoloration giving parts of the coat a brown tinge, or "tarnish," instead of silver. Discoloration of this kind often shows on the head and legs. In smoke British Shorthairs, i.e. non-tabbies, the poor silver coloring produces something quite different: a cat where you have to look very hard for the pale contrasting undercoat. These cats are also known as "low-grade smokes." Other discolorations which occur in silver tabbies and tipped British Shorthairs are often only temporary. They affect mainly the head, and occur in suckling queens and in wet, cold weather. The temporary discoloration of the coat linked with such conditions is called "rufism."

Eye colors

Only tipped British Shorthairs with green eyes are recognized. In silver tabbies, the eye color may be green or orange. Yet again, cats with orange eyes and cats with green eyes are not of course mated to each other. Smokes belong to the self-colored group of cats, and so always have orange eyes.

Silver tabbies

Silver tabbies are agouti cats, and show their tabby pattern over a silver undercoat. About half of each hair, from the root upwards, is unpigmented. Silver tabby British Shorthairs, especially black silver spotted and blotched tabbies, have been very popular in recent years, for one reason because of their appearance in advertising campaigns featuring cats.

It is not easy to breed good silver tabbies. A considerable number of polygenetically determined factors have to be taken into account;

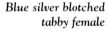

Blue silver blotched tabby female

Black silver blotched tabby; the pattern can be clearer.

Black silver blotched tabby male

these factors will decide whether the cat does or does not have clearly patterned markings combined with a magnificent silvery white undercoat. Furthermore, the animal's physique has to satisfy the standard and be of the correct cobby type. All in all, many different ideals are involved, and it is extremely difficult to unite them in a single cat.

Smokes

Black silver shell male

When the inhibitor gene affects a self-colored cat, the cat is called a smoke. In the ideal smoke one-third to a half of every hair is unpigmented from the root upwards. Sometimes it is not easy to see whether kittens are smokes or not. Indications are a head of a lighter color (with "spectacles") and lighter hairs on the underside

of the tail and round the neck. However, the silver can fade temporarily during puberty, returning only when the cat is fully grown. Breeding a good smoke is not simple, and is one reason why this variety is not often bred. In practice, most smokes are born from heterozygous silver tabbies. If the parents have green eyes – as they usually do – the kitten will not satisfy the standard. Smokes, being self colors, ought to have orange eyes.

Black silver shaded male

Tipped British Shorthairs

Tipped British Shorthairs are in point of fact silver tabbies. Through generations of selection for cats with the faintest of tabby patterns, animals were finally bred in which the tabby pattern formerly present had faded to a kind of dark veil over the silver undercoat. The lightest version of tipping is called "shell" or "chinchilla"; cats with darker tipping are called "shaded." In shell cats only one-eighth of each hair is pigmented; in shaded cats about one-third of each hair. Since the amount of tipping is polygenetically determined, shell and shaded kittens can be born in the same litter. If the parent animals with tipping are not heterozygous for silver, non-silver kittens can be born. These animals, which have a warm golden brown undercoat, are called "golden shell" or "golden shaded." The expressive dark "mascara lines" round the eyes are an attractive feature of the silver varieties; the nose leather is outlined in the same way. Tipped British Shorthairs can of course be bred in the full range of coat colors. Normally cats in this color group are crossed only among themselves, but there is sometimes an outcross with a green-eyed silver tabby in order to broaden the bloodline.

P. 117:
*red colorpointed
male*

15 COLOR-POINTED BRITISH SHORTHAIRS

Colorpointed British Shorthairs

One of the newer varieties in the color range is the colorpointed cat. The recessive partial albino "cs" factor restricts the development of color to the animal's extremities. A typical feature of this factor is that the color comes through only on the cooler parts of the body; a colorpointed animal will keep changing color slightly all its life, with the main coat becoming slightly darker as time goes on, since the older cat grows the less able it is to maintain its own body heat at the right level. The markings of the colorpointed British Shorthair are at their most attractive when the cat is about two years old. They have then had time to come through well, and the contrast with the main coat will still be distinct.

Colorpointed cats are always born white, and the color of the points comes in gradually. The darkest point colorings show first, but it is

This older seal tortie colorpointed queen illustrates the way in which colorpointed cats can change color during their lives.

Young blue colorpointed male

Chocolate silver tabby colorpointed male

118 COLORPOINTED BRITISH SHORTHAIRS

Chocolate color-pointed kitten

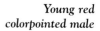
Young red colorpointed male

clear what all the point colors are within eight weeks of birth. These cats occur in a wide color range, from the classic seal colorpointd BSH to the latest varieties of silver tabby colorpointed cats.

Eye color

The eyes of colorpointed cats should be deep blue, but so far this is just the ideal. Most of them have eyes of a light to medium blue. Initially, animals with orange eyes were those mainly used in the breeding of the colorpointed British Shorthair, and in the second generation of colorpointed kittens eye color changed to the desired pale blue. At the moment eye color is being improved by crossing with green-eyed British Shorthairs, with the aim of achieving deeper blue eyes in colorpointed cats.

16 LIST OF COLORS

Self colors, including white and smoke versions (orange eyes)
Black, chocolate, cinnamon, blue, lilac, fawn, black tortie, chocolate tortie, cinnamon tortie, blue-cream, lilac-cream, fawn-cream, red, cream. White with orange eyes, white with one orange and one blue eye (odd-eyed), white with blue eyes. Black smoke, chocolate smoke, cinnamon smoke, blue smoke, lilac smoke, fawn smoke, black tortie smoke, chocolate tortie smoke, cinnamon tortie smoke, blue-cream smoke, lilac-cream smoke, fawn-cream smoke, red smoke, cream smoke.

Tabbies (orange eyes)
Black blotched/striped/spotted/ticked, chocolate blotched/striped/spotted/ticked, cinnamon blotched/striped/spotted/ticked, blue blotched/striped/spotted/ticked, lilac blotched/striped/spotted/ticked, fawn blotched/striped/spotted/ticked, black tortie blotched/striped/spotted/ticked, chocolate tortie blotched/striped/spotted/ticked, cinnamon tortie blotched/striped/spotted/ticked, blue-cream blotched/striped/spotted/ticked, lilac-cream blotched/striped/spotted/ticked, fawn-cream blotched/striped/spotted/ticked, red blotched/striped/spotted/ticked, cream blotched/striped/spotted/ticked.

Black silver blotched/striped/spotted/ticked, chocolate silver blotched/striped/spotted/ticked, cinnamon silver blotched/striped/spotted/ticked, blue silver blotched/striped/spotted/ticked, lilac silver blotched/striped/spotted/ticked, fawn silver blotched/striped/spotted/ticked, black tortie silver blotched/striped/spotted/ticked, chocolate tortie silver blotched/striped/spotted/ticked; cinnamon tortie silver blotched/striped/spotted/ticked, blue-cream silver blotched/striped/spotted/ticked, lilac-cream silver blotched/striped/spotted/ticked, fawn-cream silver blotched/striped/spotted/ticked, red silver blotched/striped/spotted/ticked, cream silver blotched/striped/spotted/ticked.

Silver and golden tabbies (green eyes)
Black silver blotched/striped/spotted/ticked, chocolate silver blotched/striped/spotted/ticked, cinnamon silver blotched/striped/spotted/ticked, blue silver blotched/striped/spotted/ticked, lilac silver blotched/striped/spotted/ticked, fawn silver

blotched/striped/spotted/ticked, black tortie silver
blotched/striped/spotted/ticked, chocolate tortie silver
blotched/striped/spotted/ticked, blue-cream silver
blotched/striped/spotted/ticked, lilac-cream silver
blotched/striped/spotted/ticked, fawn-cream silver
blotched/striped/spotted/ticked, red silver
blotched/striped/spotted/ticked, cream silver blotched/striped/spotted/ticked.

Black golden blotched/striped/spotted/ticked, chocolate golden
blotched/striped/spotted/ticked, cinnamon golden
blotched/striped/spotted/ticked, blue golden blotched/striped/spotted/ticked, lilac golden blotched/striped/spotted/ticked, fawn golden
blotched/striped/spotted/ticked, black tortie golden
blotched/striped/spotted/ticked, chocolate tortie golden
blotched/striped/spotted/ticked, cinnamon tortie golden
blotched/striped/spotted/ticked, blue-cream golden
blotched/striped/spotted/ticked, lilac-cream golden
blotched/striped/spotted/ticked, fawn-cream golden
blotched/striped/spotted/ticked, red golden
blotched/striped/spotted/ticked, cream golden blotched/striped/spotted/ticked.

Tipped British Shorthairs (shell/chinchilla and shaded), silver and golden (green eyes)

Black silver shell/shaded, chocolate silver shell/shaded, cinnamon silver shell/shaded, lilac silver shell/shaded, black tortie silver shell/shaded, chocolate tortie silver shell/shaded, cinnamon tortie silver shell/shaded, blue-cream silver shell/shaded, lilac-cream silver shell/shaded, fawn-cream silver shell/shaded, red silver shell/shaded, cream silver shell/shaded, black golden shell/shaded, chocolate golden shell/shaded, cinnamon golden shell/shaded, blue golden shell/shaded, lilac golden shell/shaded, fawn golden shell/shaded, black tortie golden shell/shaded, chocolate tortie golden shell/shaded, cinnamon tortie golden shell/shaded, blue-cream golden shell/shaded, lilac-cream golden shell/shaded, fawn-cream golden shell/shaded, red golden shell/shaded, cream golden shell/shaded.

Bi-colors, Harlequins and Van patterns (orange eyes, sometimes odd-eyed or blue)

Black and white, chocolate and white, cinnamon and white, blue and white, lilac and white, fawn and white, black tortie and white, chocolate tortie and white, cinnamon tortie and white, blue-cream and white, lilac-cream and white, fawn-cream and white, red and white, cream and white.

Black blotched/striped/spotted/ticked tabby and white, chocolate
blotched/striped/spotted/ticked tabby and white, cinnamon
blotched/striped/spotted/ticked tabby and white, blue
blotched/striped/spotted/ticked tabby and white, lilac
blotched/striped/spotted/ticked tabby and white, fawn

blotched/striped/spotted/ticked tabby and white, black tortie blotched/striped/spotted/ticked tabby and white, chocolate tortie blotched/striped/spotted/ticked tabby and white, cinnamon tortie blotched/striped/spotted/ticked tabby and white, blue-cream blotched/striped/spotted/ticked tabby and white, lilac-cream blotched/striped/spotted/ticked tabby and white, fawn-cream blotched/striped/spotted/ticked tabby and white, red blotched/striped/spotted/ticked tabby and white, cream blotched/striped/spotted/ticked tabby and white.

Colorpointed British Shorthairs (blue-eyed)
Seal colorpointed, chocolate colorpointed, cinnamon colorpointed, blue colorpointed, lilac colorpointed, fawn colorpointed, red color-pointed, cream colorpointed, seal tortie colorpointed, chocolate tortie colorpointed, cinnamon tortie colorpointed, blue-cream colorpointed, lilac-cream colorpointed, fawn-cream colorpointed, seal tabby color-pointed, chocolate tabby colorpointed, cinnamon tabby colorpointed, blue tabby colorpointed, lilac tabby colorpointed, fawn tabby color-pointed, seal tortie tabby colorpointed, chocolate tortie tabby color-pointed, cinnamon tortie tabby colorpointed, blue-cream tabby colorpointed, lilac-cream tabby colorpointed, fawn-cream tabby color-pointed, red tabby colorpointed, cream tabby colorpointed.

Seal smoke colorpointed, chocolate smoke colorpointed, cinnamon smoke colorpointed, blue smoke colorpointed, lilac smoke colorpoint-

An inquisitive blue male

ed, fawn smoke colorpointed, seal tortie smoke colorpointed, chocolate tortie smoke colorpointed, cinnamon tortie smoke colorpointed, blue-cream smoke colorpointed, lilac-cream smoke colorpointed, fawn-cream smoke colorpointed, red smoke colorpointed, cream smoke colorpointed. Seal silver tabby colorpointed, chocolate silver tabby colorpointed, cinnamon silver tabby colorpointed, blue silver tabby colorpointed, lilac silver tabby colorpointed, fawn silver tabby colorpointed, seal tortie silver tabby colorpointed, chocolate tortie silver tabby colorpointed, cinnamon tortie silver tabby colorpointed, blue-cream silver tabby colorpointed, lilac-cream silver tabby colorpointed, fawn-cream silver tabby colorpointed, red silver tabby colorpointed, cream silver tabby colorpointed.

Seal silver shaded colorpointed, chocolate silver shaded colorpointed, cinnamon silver shaded colorpointed, blue silver shaded colorpointed, lilac silver shaded colorpointed, fawn silver shaded colorpointed, seal tortie silver shaded colorpointed, chocolate tortie silver shaded colorpointed, cinnamon tortie silver shaded colorpointed, blue-cream silver shaded colorpointed, lilac-cream silver shaded colorpointed, fawn-cream silver shaded colorpointed, red silver shaded colorpointed, cream silver shaded colorpointed.

Seal golden shaded colorpointed, chocolate golden shaded colorpointed, cinnamon golden shaded colorpointed, blue golden shaded colorpointed, lilac golden shaded colorpointed, fawn golden shaded colorpointed, seal tortie golden shaded colorpointed, chocolate tortie golden shaded colorpointed, cinnamon tortie golden shaded colorpointed, cinnamon tortie golden shaded colorpointed, blue-cream golden shaded colorpointed, lilac-cream golden shaded colorpointed, fawn-cream golden shaded colorpointed, red golden shaded colorpointed, cream golden shaded colorpointed.

*In view of the great number of colors, and for the sake of clarity, we have chosen to employ a uniform terminology out of the various versions in current use. Other terms for the colors will be found in the Glossary.

17 GLOSSARY

A

Agouti gene: under the influence of this dominant gene (A), the tabby pattern carried by every cat becomes visible.

B

Bi-colors: term for the group of cats which shows a certain amount of white in the coat as well as a self-color. Bi-colors, Van pattern and Harlequin cats all come into this group.
Blue: dilute version of black, which appears when the recessive gene for dilute coloring (d) is present.
Blue-cream: dilute version of tortie, also called blue tortie.
Blotched: one of the main tabby patterns, also called Classic.
British Variant: term used for the longhaired cats occasionally born to British Shorthair parents.
Brown tabby: misleading term for black tabby, still in use.

C

Chinchilla: alternative term for shell, used for British Shorthairs with tipping which occupies only about one-eighth of their hairs.
Chocolate: chocolate brown coat coloring, a mutation of black. The dilute version of chocolate is lilac.
Chocolate tortie: a mingled pattern of chocolate and red hairs.
Cinnamon: a mutation of black. The dilute version of cinnamon is fawn.
Classic: American term for a blotched tabby.
Colorpoint, colorpointed: the recessive mutation (cs) of complete coloring (C). The cs gene originates with the Siamese breed, and was bred via Persians into the British Shorthair.
Cream: dilute version of red, which appears when the recessive gene for dilute coloring (d) is present.
Cross-breeding: the crossing of two animals of different breeds, for instance the occasional introduction of a Persian into British Shorthair stock.

D

Dilution: appears when the recessive gene for dilution (d) is doubly present. Under its influence the pigment particles in the hairs cluster together, making the coat look optically paler.
Dominant gene: dominant genes are those which are always evident in the phenotype, and thus even when present only in single form determine the outward qualities of the cat.

E

Eumelanins: pigment particles causing the color of the coat to be black and all the colors derived from it (blue, chocolate, lilac, cinnamon).

Extremities: a collective term for those parts of the cat which are colored, in contrast to the pale main coat, in colorpointed cats: legs, face, tail and ears, and the scrotum in males.

F
Fawn: dilute form of cinnamon which appears when the recessive gene for dilution (d) is doubly present.
Fawn-cream: a mingled pattern of cream and fawn hairs, also known as fawn tortie. A dilute form of cinnamon tortie which appears when the recessive gene for dilution (d) is doubly present.

G
Gene: the carrier of a hereditary characteristic.
Genotype: the cat's inherited set of genes. It can differ from the phenotype.
Ghost markings: faint tabby markings on non-agouti cats, most clearly visible in kittens.
Golden: collective term for green-eyed non-silver cats descended from a line of green-eyed silver ancestors.

H
Harlequin: coat pattern in which the only color is on top of the head, the fully colored tail, and a maximum of three colored patches on the body.
Heterozygous: not true-breeding. The term is used when the cat has two different genes for a particular characteristic. The cat's phenotype then differs from its genotype.
Homozygous: true-breeding. The term is used when both genes for a particular characteristic are the same.

I
Inhibitor gene: dominant gene which inhibits the pigmentation of a part of the coat from the root of the hair, creating a silver undercoat.
Inbreeding: crossing closely related animals (matings between brother and sister, mother and son, half-brother and half-sister).

K
Kink: deviation in the tail vertebrae, a polygenetically inherited fault affecting appearance only.

L
Lilac: dilute form of chocolate which appears when the recessive gene for dilution (d) is doubly present.
Lilac-cream: also called lilac tortie. A mingled pattern of cream and lilac hairs.
Line breeding: another term for inbreeding, often used for matings between less closely related animals, for instance

grandfather to grandchild, or cousin to cousin.

M
Mackerel: another term for a striped tabby.
Mutation: spontaneously occurring change in the genetic material which is passed on to the cat's progeny.

N
Non-agouti: term used when the visible display of the tabby pattern present is suppressed.

O
Odd-eyed: a cat with eyes of two different colors (one blue, one orange), occurring in self white cats and cats with a considerable amount of white in their coats.
Outcross: the crossing of two animals which have no or very few ancestors in common within the breed.

P
Phaeomelanin: pigment particles causing a red coat color.
Phenotype: the visible outward appearance of the cat.
Pinch: indentation behind the whisker pads; an undesirable fault in the head of the British Shorthair.
Points: the darker colored extremities in colorpointed cats.

R
Recessive gene: gene which can reveal itself in the phenotype only when the kitten inherits it from both parents.

S
Seal: another term for black, in use for colorpointed cats, where it occurs as very dark brown.
Shaded: tabby pattern which has faded, under the influence of generations of selective breeding, to a shadow over the ground colors; the darker form of chinchilla or shell.
Shell: another term for chinchilla.
Smoke: non-agouti cat with a silver undercoat produced by the inhibitor gene.
Spotted: one of the four forms of tabby.
Stop: indentation in the nose-line, breaking the slope.
Stud jowls: strongly developed jowls in entire males, hormonally determined; this feature wears off after castration.
Stud tail: a sticky brown substance on the tail of an entire male, caused by the sebaceous gland when it secretes excessive sebum.

T
Tabby: coat pattern expressing itself through the presence of the agouti gene. There are four different possible forms of tabby: blotched, striped, spotted, and ticked.
Ticked: one of the four tabby patterns. The near-absence of

markings is typical of the ticked tabby. The coat consists of hairs with two to three dark bands on each, as in the wild rabbit. Stripes are only faintly visible on the legs and tail.

Tipped: term for the chinchilla or shell British Shorthair. Only the lighter form is bred in the United Kingdom; while the darker (shaded) form is also bred on the continent of Europe.

Tipping: the phenomenon whereby the cat's real color is still visible only at the tips of the hairs. The lighter form is called shell or chinchilla, the rather darker form is called shaded.

Tortie: tortoise shell cat, usually shortened to tortie: cat with a mingled pattern of eumelanins and phaeomelanins.

Tortie tabby: a cat with a coat combining tabby and tortie markings.

V

Van pattern: cat with one or two colored patches on the head, a colored tail and a white body.

A pair of black silver shaded kittens lying in wait

18 USEFUL ADDRESSES

The Governing Council
of the Cat Fancy
4–6 Penel Orlieu
Bridgwater
Somerset TA6 3PG
United Kingdom

The Cat Association
CA Central Office
Mill House
Letcombe Regis
Oxon OX12 9JD
United Kingdom

The British Shorthair Cat Club
Hon. Secretary: Mrs M. Coleman
Blean-Y-Glyn
Llawr-Y-Glyn
Caersws
Powys SY17 5RJ
United Kingdom

The Cat Fanciers' Association Inc.
P.O. Box 1005
Manasquan
NJ 08736-10805
U.S.A.

19 ACKNOWLEDGEMENTS AND PHOTOGRAPHIC CREDITS

All the photographs were taken by Esther Verhoef except for those on pp. 34, 35, 42, 42, 60, 72, 75 left and 105, which were taken by Marijke van Leeuwn; 32 below, 51, 68, 69 below, 78 and 76 by Joost Schwartz; 32 above and 98 left by Henny Bok; 26 above and 98 right by Cora Swierts; and 110 and 113 below by Monique Knook. The black-and-white photos are from *The Book of the Cat* (1903), by Frances Simpson.

The author and publisher would like to thank Mevrouw Henny Bok and Mimy Sluiter for looking through this manuscript. Their comments have been incorporated. In addition, the author would like to thank all the breeders and owners who were kind enough to let their cats be photographed. The majority of the cats were photographed in the homes of Joost Schwartz, Henny Bok, Marit van Ewijk, Mevr. I. den Hollander, and the H. van Rouij family. Thanks are also due to the veterinarian W. Kampschöer and the assistants at the veterinary practice of Zaltbommel in Zaltbommel, and the two feline models for the medical photographs.